CONVERSATIONS
WITH
MY DARK SIDE

CONVERSATIONS WITH MY DARK SIDE

Shanti Ananda

NEW FALCON PUBLICATIONS
TEMPE, ARIZONA, U.S.A.

International Standard Book Number: 1-56184-127-7

First Edition 1997

Cover Art by Denise Cuttitta

The paper used in this publication meets the minimum requirements of the American National Standard for Permanence of Paper for Printed Library Materials Z39.48-1984

Address all inquiries to:
NEW FALCON PUBLICATIONS
1739 East Broadway Road Suite 1-277
Tempe, AZ 85282 U.S.A.
(or)
1209 South Casino Center
Las Vegas, NV 89104 U.S.A.

Everyone
Has A Dark Side.
And It Is Not Necessary
To Engage It In Conversation.
Just Know That
You Are Not
Alone!!

AUTHOR'S NOTE

The events and persons in this book are real. However, to protect the privacy of individuals, I have used pseudonyms and have altered personal descriptions.

To Jeff

TABLE OF CONTENTS

PREFACE

Published in the Chicago Tribune circa 1993

Bright beady eyes stare into mine as I open the door. They are set in a young face on legs which hop from one foot to another like a sparrow, light and nervous round a bird feeder, ready for take-off.

Bedecked in chains, the tow truck squats like a big, fat bug in the driveway. Neighborhood drapes rustle with excitement. My legs feel like two wooden casings filled with cement.

"Is your husband in?" The young man looks the same age as my son.

"No." The lie pops out like a shelled pea. My husband is in the office at the back of the house, described in the Realtor's literature as Sun-Room, 10′ × 14′.

"Are you his wife?"

No, I just happened to be passing, saw the front door open and decided to play home-owner for a few hours. "Yes," I answer.

"I've come for the Mercedes and if you don't let me have it, I will call the police!" The sentence shoots across the space like a racket ball straight to my heart, bounces up to my throat and lodges like a great lump of porridge. I cannot return a word.

Looking at him from a body no longer mine, I hear a voice say, "Just a minute, I'll contact my husband on the phone." The screen door swishes behind me, a flimsy barrier against the chained pariah silently waiting in the driveway.

Legs carry me down the hall, through the kitchen, past white counter tops where two coffee mugs happily steam, past the round oak table strewn with the morning Tribune, past the white railed division of the family room, past Millie snoring softly in her basket, and out through sliding glass doors into the office.

"They've come for the car," I croak.

13

My husband's face remains fixed while color drains from his skin like a rip-tide. We trade expressions until our faces look the same. He picks up the phone and talks to Mike at the Credit Corp., but we all know pleasant phone techniques will not replace hard cash. Unable to witness defeat, my legs carry me back to the front door to see what the tow truck is doing.

I smile at the young face whose unfortunate job it is to repossess other people's possessions. For a second it catches him off guard. "My husband is calling the guy at Mercedes."

"I'm not leaving without the car!" His eyes are bright with dramatic tension.

"I understand that, but we're trying to see if there is any way out of this mess."

"I will call the police if I have to."

I see it all: flashing cars, orange jackets roping off the area, and local paparazzi beating down the bushes for a photo opportunity. Silent gaper's whispering, "they looked normal, but..."

"Don't worry," I assure him. "We're seeing if we can fix it, that's all."

"Do what you like, but I'm not leaving without the car."

"Give me a minute will you—please?"

He nods, walks back to the tow truck and waits. "If my kids ever ask, 'When did middle age hit you?' I will say, 'While standing on my front porch staring into the face of a boy the same age as you, and feeling like I had just been caught stealing.'"

I did not bother waiting for the result of the phone conversation. I knew we did not have the $1,700 car payments necessary to keep the Mercedes. I walk to the family room and open the door leading to the garage; cold air with a faint tinge of gasoline hits me like an oil rag.

The car waits, black and shiny with an understatement of chrome. The heavy door silently swings open to reveal an interior of gray leather perfectly patterned with pin sized holes that exhale the smell of upper income. Holding a plastic Jewel bag in one hand, I shovel my car paraphernalia into it with the other. Lipsticks, pens, eyebrow tweezers, hand cream, tissues, coins, brushes, cassette tapes, pile in with the bustle of indiscriminate garbage.

Pulling down the front compartment I collect repair and maintenance receipts and a five dollar bill left there for emergencies; only one thousand, six hundred and ninety-five dollars too short! Finally, I reach behind the front seat into the back pockets and remove a Chicago street map. Taking the rolled umbrella off the back window, I close the door quietly behind me. I feel like a traitor. We bought the car two years earlier when the business was prosperous; we promised to pay and care for it until it was ours; it was like giving a teenager up for adoption.

My husband walks into the garage, his face tells the story—the car is history! At the front door, I call in a voice polite but distant, "you can take it away now."

Now that the car is philosophically totaled, I want it gone as quickly as possible. Running back to the garage, I press the door opener. Daylight floods over the defenseless vehicle. "Are the keys in?" asks the young man.

"Yes," I smile. "This is such a relief."

He gives me a quizzical look like I have just given him $20. "You'll get the car back when you make the payments," he says.

"No." Shaking my head I explain, "We never could afford it really, I'm glad it's going." He half-smiles in acknowledgment of human frailty, then backs the car out. Pushing the garage door button, I am inside the house before the door is closed.

Like a broken mirror, we have seven years bad credit—and still have to pay the difference between what the car sells at auction and what we owe.

Friends and I often joke about the meaning of life; I used to laugh and say, "There is none!" Now I think the meaning of life changes depending where you are at the time. For me, the meaning is not to give up when bad times hit.

What I need right now I think, is a good book. Maybe David Copperfield, particularly the bit where Charles Dickens has Mr. Micawber say, "Annual income twenty shillings, annual expenditure nineteen shillings and six pence, result happiness. Annual income twenty shillings, annual expenditure twenty pounds and sixpence, result misery!"

THE DAWN OF RECKONING

Two Years Later

I am sitting upstairs in a room too small to hold a bed. The door hangs thick with old paint like blobs of mascara on thin lashes. A panel is replaced by glass jammed in with floor tacks and wire. One small gummed label reads: "PARENTAL ADVISORY EXPLICIT LYRICS". A torn star the size of a dime smiles bleakly from the top right corner.

Two sash windows on my left are nailed shut. A dusty moth with its feet in the air rests on the sill. If the room were a person it would have rheumy eyes, broken teeth and two feet of hair wrapped round a balding head. Not a sight to inspire the poetry muse within—but oh, what a great place to seduce my dark side!

The walls of my writing room are pressed wood painted white. They are bare, save for a four inch hole made by an architect with bull frog eyes who recorded our dreams on thick scrolls. Spiders dance on them at night in the cellar.

When we can pay the $1,200 to Lake Forest City Council for the building permit, our wonderful old rickety house will be remodeled. The porch, held up by a car jack, will become a gourmet kitchen with center isle—the stained steel sink, stainless as God intended, and I will present sumptuous meals to mouths poised above over-stuffed forks.

My determination that this will succeed is augmented by the fact that you are reading this. For this is a story about my struggle with the dark side—that gross, demonic monster, which boils around my mind with suppurating sores sprouting from a hideous body. Its agenda is survival and until my vision quest two years ago, when my dark side appeared from out of a hollow tree (about which I will tell you later), I denied its existence. So let me introduce you, "ah there you are, please say a few words."

"Fuck off and stop writing stupid stuff."

"Make me stop."

At this point the woman feels cold. Her fingers become blue tinged icicles tapping across frozen numbered peaks. Cold is on her mind. It becomes so strong that she rises from her seat and switches the heater to *high*. Only then, does she realize she has stopped writing! At least she knows her opponent. Knows it resides within the vast unconscious space of her mind waiting to blot out the sun. The woman speaks to her dark side again. "So you think you got the better of me?"

"I know I did you silly, old fat cow. You overweight cock sucker."

"That's where you're wrong, I don't do that."

"Now why is that?"

"It reminds me of egg white: stringy blobs of gluttonous jelly."

"So you're scared?"

"Maybe."

"What does hubby think?"

"He doesn't."

"Sure?"

"Yes. No. I mean yes." Is her dark side helping her overcome fear? She reads that fear can manifest in the body and cause CANCER!

"Aha! The most dastardly word in your vocabulary." Her dark side knows every fear.

"Yes."

"You've had CANCER once, and you think you've got it again."

"Right."

"So you have."

"How do you know?"

"I know everything. I scan your body for the festering places where fear makes its home."

"I'm not listening."

"Oh but you are. You want to know about your CANCER. If you have it, and how far it has spread."

"So tell me the worst. Speak the unspeakable."

"It's about to manifest in your colon. That's why you wake up every morning with a pain in your left side."

"Is there anything I can do about it?"

"No."

"You seem quite happy about this!"

"Don't care one way or the other."

"But if I die, you die too."

"You don't get it, sweetie. I'm not part of you. I don't belong to you. As soon as you die, I go to another human being and torment them to death."

"Is that your purpose in life?"

"My purpose is to bring about the downfall of the human race."

"Why?"

"Because you're a selfish mass of marauding mind masturbators. You have made a world where everything must be bigger, better and faster. You're a waste of energy. Do you know that energy is a carefully preserved secret of the universe?"

"No, but I've read about quarks, they're a lot of nothing spinning fast that don't exist until we direct our attention on them. I figure, that since we're all made up of quarks, we don't even exist until someone takes notice of us. It's like we're all linked together on a big internet, but we're too scared to hook up the modem."

The woman has experienced conversations where she does not exist. Mourned the loss of a sentence drowned in an avalanche of louder and more important sounding words. Her husband says her timing is off—that she should wait for a lull in the conversation. She has noticed however, that the people who are listened to, do not bother to wait.

The woman reads books like *A Brief History of Time* by Stephen Hawking. She summarizes each chapter like a Rhodes scholar. Yet, alone in the wilderness with nothing but the clothes on her back, she couldn't make a half-watt light bulb glow; the most dimwitted firefly would outshine her! At a push, she could sharpen a small stone to a rough point. But in the end she would be forced to eat evil looking berries, dead beetles and slug *a la* raw. Within hours, she'd wish for a fraction of what her ancestors, the small-brained, hairy ones knew.

The woman lifts her shoulders until she is wearing them like earrings. She is after all, a vegetarian, a non-drinker, a yogi, a swami priest! She gives change to street people in Chicago. At

O'Hare she drops a dollar bill into the saxophone case of the player who blows jazz at the parking elevator. One time she almost dropped a twenty dollar bill into the hat of an old homeless person, but as she drew nearer the smell got stronger and he seemed less deserving, so she passed him by. Still, she teaches meditation and Hatha Yoga—what more can a civilized person do?

"I sometimes wonder about the strange and weird people in the world. Only this morning I read about, *The Man Who Mistook His Wife For A Hat* by Oliver Sacks. The man was a professor of music who slowly lost his mind until one day he reached across to his wife's head, and tried to put it on his own head as if it were a hat! The image frightens me."

"Why?" The dark side lusts after fear.

"Because my husband and I work for ourselves. We have no security. No savings. No collateral. We have debts."

"How much?"

"About..." Like most people in debt, the woman does not know the amount to which she is indebted. Grudgingly, she begins to count. "I have three major credit cards with roughly, $5,000, $3,000 and $2,000 outstanding."

"That's $10,000."

"And school fees."

"Still rescuing the two brats eh? Make the little bastards pay for themselves."

"Only another $8,000 then we've finished," she said.

"Sucker! Those kids will be on your back for the rest of your natural life. And when they have kids," the dark side pauses for effect, "guess who will be buying Jumping Jehoshaphat sneakers at over a hundred bucks a pop! Get real lady, wake up and be conscious! But you won't listen, so carry on with your debt list, why don't you."

"We owe $500 to one printer, and $3,500 to another."

"The one who sent the fax: 'Move out of Lake Forest so you can pay your debts like other decent people!'"

The woman tugs on her lashes; reality is a painful sight. If she totals all her debt, it will become real. If it becomes real, it will have to be paid. She glances at the door and thinks about foraging for food.

"Go on, do it."

"Do what?"

"Don't play games with me, sweetie. I'm inside your head, remember? Go to the kitchen and stuff your fat face. There's cereal, cheese, bananas, frozen Cherry Garcia yogurt, recently renamed, Bury Garcia!" chuckles the dark side malevolently. "You could even shuffle over the train tracks and buy a rich, cream, chocolate Easter egg."

The woman's mouth waters like an underground cave. Saliva forms into droplets and splashes around her tongue like a car wash. She envisions the Lake Forester Police Blotter: LOCAL FOOD JUNKIE DROWNS IN SPITTLE. She swallows. But still, the need for sugar...

"Why do I need chocolate so much?"

"To sweeten your dark mind."

"I don't have a dark mind."

"Like I said, to sweeten your dark mind. I'm in there, I know how dark it gets."

She looks out the window. Cars old and new carry people to jobs, to market, to Starbucks. People with missions. People with lives. Does she have a life? What if her whole life is a dream and she wakes up to find herself dead? What if then, the realization hits: she could have done and been anything she wanted?

She recalls a story of some people taking a tour of heaven who come upon a vast area bursting with more things than the major Trumpster, Donald could buy for Mar-a-lago: swimming pools, clothes, yachts, tennis courts, designer toothpicks, their eyes boggle, "What's all this?" they ask.

"The dreams that people gave up on," came the reply.

"I don't need chocolate," says the woman.

"It's your choice," answers the dark side.

"I've noticed something about our relationship," chuckles the woman.

"We don't have a relationship. I tell you what to do, and you do it. I am the all seeing, all powerful, omnipotent, omnipresent one."

"You talk as if you are God," she snorts.

"I am God."

"I don't think so! God isn't a prick like you."

"Says who? If God is everything, then God is also evil."

The conversation takes a thirty second hiatus, after which the woman says, "God is separate and apart from evil; God in one corner, Satan in the other."

The dark side, bored with God says, "Let's go back to your cancer. What's the point of writing this book when you are about to die? Indulge yourself. Eat chocolate. Loosen your bra, put your feet up. Watch soaps. You deserve the best."

"You'll tell me next that because I've *worked out* today, I can have all the chocolate I want!"

"So you can. Remember Brian in your office? He runs twice a day, eats anything he wants and has six beers a night. He keeps his weight down—you can too!"

The woman ignores the voice. "I owe $22,000 plus three car payments totaling $18,000 and a mortgage of $100,000."

"You can't count the mortgage."

"My husband wants to pay it off."

The dark side mimics her in a sing-song whining voice, "My husband wants to pay it off!"

The woman continues the count. "$140,000. Add $60,000 for remodeling. That makes $200,000!"

"You won't get that kind of money in a million years."

The woman feels a third presence. She jumps. "Oh-my-God. I didn't see you there."

This is a complete lie. A few minutes earlier she saw her daughter's red Fiat pull up the drive but it's the way she dramatizes her life. Small lies. Pretend games, as if she is a child playing make believe, forty years too late.

The role of being startled is so strong that for a moment her daughter's face becomes that of a robber. Then her daughter speaks, "Hi momma." The woman takes in the reality of her daughter's beautiful face. Silva is 26 years old, a Harvard graduate who has just returned from a trip to Australia. Her long black hair shines with sunlight and untold experiences.

"Hi my darling. Come in."

The dark side interrupts the conversation by talking inside the woman's head, "You think you can get away without mentioning AIDS?"

"It's got nothing to do with the book."

"You're trying to edit me, dumb fuck?"

The woman remains silent.

"Hey nickel-head. If you want to talk with me you have to accept everything I say. I am a voice that can't be stilled."

She thinks of the horrendous murderers on TV. Moronic masks with mouth holes saying, "The voice in my head made me do it, it was God. It's all His fault!"

The woman turns the dark voice off, looks at her daughter and says. "Sit on my knee."

She loves it when her daughter sits on her lap. Sometimes her husband will do it. But he feels such an idiot—it rarely happens.

Silva sits on her lap, "Mom, everywhere I go I hear about AIDS. They were even talking about it at work last night. Do you think it's an omen?"

"Of course not. It's the same when you buy a new car, suddenly every car on the road is like yours. You are just conscious of AIDS right now, that's all." The woman speaks with a bravado she does not feel.

Since getting home, Silva has worked as a childcare counselor at a half-way house for girls aged 12 to 16. It's a big responsibility helping shape children's lives, but like many childcare situations, the pay is minimal; even graduating *summa cum laude* doesn't up the ante!

Her daughter is learning about another dark side. Girls with no place to go. Girls who have been pried from abusive situations like rape, incest or beatings. One girl has an SOS out on her. Not the shipwrecked cry of mariners in need of help as in, *Save Our Souls*. But the modern equivalent as in, *Shoot On Sight*. And this, because the girl had stolen crack from a gang member.

Another girl has been repeatedly raped by her mother's boyfriend, forced to live with him and star in his porno movies; she is 14 years old. The girl is medicated with the same drug they recommend for PMS—the new Valium of the 90's. She rarely has flashbacks now, and when they do happen, she bangs her head against the wall until she becomes unconscious again.

"So how was last night?" asks the woman.

"Okay. It was the first night on my own."

"On your own?"

"There's usually another counselor there, but if one of us takes the girls on an activity like skating or swimming, the other one is on her own."

The woman lets go of rape images and knife attacks in dark parking lots. That's another thing about the job, the hours are so long, sometimes Silva works sixteen hour shifts and doesn't finish until 2:00AM.

"Have you still got your mace and that electronic screaming thing?"

"Aw mom, I'm okay!"

"But do you have it?"

"Yes!"

"And you'll remember to scream 'FIRE' instead of 'HELP' if you're attacked?"

"Yes mom!" Silva sighs and wonders if she will be treated like an infant for the rest of her life. She doesn't know that when she was in Australia her mother's mind often screamed the unspeakable. It happened mostly when her brain was in neutral: brushing teeth or pumping gas, the word MURDER would flash across her mind like a Coke billboard on an empty freeway.

It was the dog's fault to begin with. She chewed Silva's passport and visa. Then the airline reservation got canceled. A few days later a United States Postal Services plastic bag arrived with a torn envelope from the Passport Office inside. The contents: presumably the replacement passport and visa, were missing. If the woman could have tied the sleeves behind her back, she would have donned a straight jacket. Finally, a psychic friend of hers casually said, "Do you think the universe is trying to send her a message? Maybe she isn't meant to go to Australia!"

With the buoyancy of an ego that can't admit to family screw ups the woman had replied, "Oh no, she'll be fine!" But it was too late, the thought seed had already sprouted. If her daughter went to Australia she would be murdered!

When her daughter came home safe and sound, the dreaded premonition immediately left of its own accord. But then Silva told her about the unprotected sex incident and the premonition zoomed back into focus, only this time, the murderer changed from a person to a virus.

Into the silence Silva pops a short sentence that she knows will illicit a response, "I got a letter today." Silva wants her mom to drag the information from her. It's about her boyfriend Jordan. He doesn't know about the AIDS thing even though they have slept together since she got back from Australia. At university

Silva listened to AIDS patients give lectures about the importance
of safe sex, but at her age, it's hard to think that making love
without a condom is tantamount to gambling with death on a
roulette wheel.

The dark side seeps back like the smell of rotting eggs
festering in a black plastic garbage bag. As if trapped in the same
bag the woman gasps, "I have told them about safe sex you
know."

"A little fucking late for that isn't it—excuse the pun," retorts
the dark side.

"Both my children know about AIDS and safe sex. My son had
an AIDS test after he had sex with a Swede on his European tour.
They think they're bullet proof—it's not my fault."

"So who's fault is it?"

"Nobody's fault—everything is perfect the way it is."

"Tell that to someone dying from AIDS!"

It's strange. The dark side talks as if it has a conscience. Is
there gray among the dark? And how does she, the woman really
feel about AIDS? What if her daughter is diagnosed with the fatal
virus? Will she still feel everything is perfect? "We all get to die.
It's the only certain thing in life, but most of us still think it's an
option—so we live our lives complaining about life!"

"On the subject of death, you created your own CANCER
because you were so angry at life, at your mother's death. You're
doing it again. You're so afraid of CANCER, you're magnetiz-
ing it into your body by your thoughts."

"Whatever!" The woman has had enough, but the dark side is
relentless.

"You create reality by your thoughts. Didn't Shakespeare say,
all the world is a stage and all the players actors?"

"Something like that."

"He was damn right, you know. All through life you get to
write your own script. You decide if it's a drama, tragedy,
romance or comedy. And you little missy, have decided to play
in a tragedy!"

"More like a black comedy actually!"

"And you aren't even directing it. You listen to other people
too much. You should start listening to your own intuition."

"How do I know what's intuition, and what's you?"

"Aha! That's a secret only you can figure out."

"Bloody marvelous!"

Her daughter is still sitting on her lap and thinking of her boyfriend. "It was easier when he was in Colorado and I was in Australia. We knew we couldn't possibly be together then. But now it's different. Now, when we could be together, we don't really know if we want to be."

There's a time lapse here. Mother and daughter go to lunch at a local eatery called Franks. They meet Steve who plays a multitude of roles: husband, father, and business partner. The waitress, a big bloused woman of indeterminate age says, "I'll be 46 on Thursday. I'm not looking forward to it."

"I'm 47," says Steve.

"But you're young," says Silva in quick defense of her dad.

"There's a woman comes in here," continues the waitress, "whose husband is 67 years old and he's gone off with a 35-year-old woman from Tahiti. I told his wife to send a photograph of the house he gave up, just to remind him of what he's missing. I mean, give me a break, what can he be doing with a woman 32 years younger?" She leans forward and whispers, "He probably can't even get it up!"

"I hope I'm still firing on all cylinders when I'm 67!" Steve defends the absentee rogue male.

The waitress brings three bowls of cheesy potato soup, an old-fashioned oatmeal with a crust of brown sugar baked on top, a mushroom omelet, one cinnamon raisin bagel and a BLT. She maneuvers them expertly around water glasses, salt and pepper shakers and small pink sachets of chemical sugar.

The woman has heard that the chemical vats used in making sugar replacements have special seals to withstand the strong corrosive effects of the ingredients, she prefers real sugar, although that too, she has read, is poisonous!

She thinks it's very hard to know what is good food anymore. It was easier for her parents. In England after the war they had ration books. Sugar and butter were luxuries. Now she reads that anything with a butter/sugar combination is trigger food for a binge, a smoking donut so to speak!

One of her spiritual directors said she should chew her food at least 20 times and savor each morsel. Chewing however, is the antithesis of a real face-stuffing-binge, so her chew rate is still in the low 5's!

"I've never been married." The waitress is speaking again. "It's hard to meet men now. All the men my age want someone at least ten years younger. And if I go for an older man—well, what would I want with some old geezer?" The four people nod as she flips her pad open and wanders off to the next table.

"This has got bacon in it!" says the woman.

"We won't tell," answers Silva.

The woman battles for a moment with her vegetarian sensibilities, then eats the last morsel of animal soup with a snorting relish that she covers with her napkin. Everyone at the table notices.

After they leave the restaurant, mother and daughter return a sweater to a local store. Her daughter has to take a pee in the employee restroom. While she is gone, the owner, Paul says, "My father is in St. Thomas, he says everyone there is very gay."

The woman frowns, surely not everyone in St. Thomas is gay? The owner continues, "I'd like to live in a place where everyone loves life."

This explains why the woman hates jokes. She is so worried about missing the punch line, it always eludes her.

"Maybe we'll go back one day. We used to live there you know. The problem is, everything is so convenient here; if I have a heart attack, at least there's a hospital round the corner!" The woman nods and he continues, "It's a good dream to have though—going back!"

The woman knows that if the dream holds out long enough, Paul will go back to St. Thomas. It's that simple. Have the dream, stick with it, and it will come true. She wonders if Paul knows that his word is law. She has attempted to have her children understand this concept, but she still hears them say things like, "My feet are killing me!" She doesn't blame them; after all, how many people go around saying, "I love my feet— they have helped me stand and walk all day long—I don't know what I would do without them!"

The other day, she heard Jim Carrey talking to the soothe-sucking face of Barbara Walters. It was his story that motivated the woman to start writing again. "Six years ago," said Jim, "I wrote a ten million dollar check to myself for acting services rendered. I put it in my wallet and carried it for that many years." Barbara urged him on with her eyes. "We did a deal a few months ago for ten million dollars, payment for doing *Mask Two!*"

It was the belief in himself that caught the woman's attention. "I used to go up to Mulholland Drive every night. Sit at the side of the road. Look at the lights and say, 'I am a popular actor. Every director wants to work with me.' And I used to open my arms and imagine things that I wanted coming my way." His eyes looked upwards as he said this. "I would stay up there until I actually believed I had all these things; then I would drive down the mountain feeling like the biggest star in Hollywood." At the end of the interview, Barbara Walters was so overcome— she couldn't speak for at least two seconds!

The woman knows that if she too believes in something that strongly, it will come true. In her wallet she carries a check in her name for ten million dollars; at the bottom it says *for writing services rendered*. She also wrote a daily affirmation: *I am 46 years old. I live in Lake Forest, Illinois. I am the author of best selling books. I have millions of dollars in the bank. I have a slim, healthy body, I am a priest and healer. I live a joy filled life. My purpose in life is to be giving.* She propped it in the bathroom cabinet beside the deodorant, and read it every morning to her mirrored image after she cleaned her teeth, but it was too long. She shortened it recently to *'My purpose in life is to be giving.'* Now she reads it when she remembers.

Mother and daughter leave the store and walk home through a misty rain that reminds her of England, homeland, ancestors and Stonehenge. Back in her writing room, she begins to keystroke. A few words later, her daughter comes in and hands her the portable phone. "I'm going to work soon," she says.

The woman puts the phone on her desk and says, "Give me a kiss then."

Her daughter pecks her cheek and says, "THERE'S SOMEONE ON THE PHONE FOR YOU MOM!" Remnants of teenage impatience seep through.

"I'm sorry, I thought you brought the phone to me because you're leaving!" In the wild, the mother would retract her claws, roll over and show her soft belly. Instead she giggles in a *please be kind to me* sort of way, picks up the phone and says, "Hello— I'm sorry, I didn't realize anybody was actually on the phone."

The dark side seeps into her day-time consciousness. "You say sorry a lot, don't you. Are you sorry for breathing too?"

The woman ignores the voice and listens to the caller, "Hi, it's me, Brenda, are you holding meditation class this week?"

"Yes."

"I'll see you then." Brenda never suspects the swami priest of jealousy. She thinks all priests are free of such lowly thoughts. She will never know the drama behind the 'thank you' card she sent.

A few days earlier the woman had taken the card out of the mail box. It was addressed to her husband but she opened it anyway. (They always open each other's mail). "Dearest Steve, thank you so much for your help. You are such a great friend." At the bottom Brenda had signed her name. A simple note, but as soon as the woman read the words 'Dearest', anger rampaged round her body like a forest fire at a pyromaniac's party. She ripped the card in two and stuffed it into the kitchen garbage along with the other junk mail.

Later, while soaking in the tub, she phones her friend Jenny to find out if 'Dearest' is an acceptable salutation in America. Coming from England where she is Mrs. to one and all, save the people she breaks wind in front of, it is hard to be objective. She says in a too normal voice, "Do you write to many people?"

"Sometimes," says Jenny wondering where the conversation is going.

"Who've you written to recently?"

The woman twiddles a piece of hair as Jenny reels off an endless list of names. Finally it ends and the woman asks, "Would you write to a male friend and start with, 'Dearest...?'"

"Who's written to Steve?" Jenny chuckles and the woman dumps a truck-load of pissed-offishness down into her lower regions—the landfill where pent-up anger is stored.

As the woman embellishes the tale, she gets out of the bath, wraps a towel round herself, takes the cordless into the kitchen, opens the garbage can and sticks her hand into piles of orange peel, melon seed and miscellaneous fruit pulp rejected earlier by the voracious juicer. The two halves of note are stuck to a pizza coupon. She does repairs with scotch tape, wipes them with an old pair of underpants now serving as a duster, and returns them to their envelope. Her timing is perfection; the door opens, her husband walks in, she hands him the envelope.

"It's torn?"

"I know!"

"Huh?" As he reads the disheveled note, the woman feels the hairs on her neck prickle as if a police car has pulled up behind her! He looks at her again with a question in his eyes.

"I was jealous!" She stares into his eyes and is relieved that he isn't annoyed. He stares back and is relieved that he's done nothing wrong. After a moment they laugh. Meanwhile, Jenny who is still on the phone hears them and says, "I can't believe you two are laughing!"

"Why not?"

"It's not serious to you?"

Steve gives her an answer she will understand, "No. I can't expect her to trust me again."

"But I do trust you," says the woman.

Neither party have been entirely faithful during their twenty-five-year marriage, but Steve has been unfaithful more times and has therefore assumed more guilt.

"If you trust me, why the jealousy?" he asks.

"I don't know."

But the woman does know and after a few seconds she 'fesses up. "It's not that I feel jealous of you having an affair with someone..."

"Right!" Her dark side knows better.

"...because I don't believe you ever will again."

"You lying little swinette!" Her dark side will not be silent.

"I just feel inadequate. When I see a young woman talking and laughing with you, I see her dreams, her hopes, her energy. I feel like an old bobbled sweater left behind at a rummage sale." She thinks of the ideal breasts displayed on glossy covers at the checkout: round and perky with youthful cleavage. "I'm jealous I don't make you feel like a young man anymore."

"Would I bring you flowers if I didn't love you AND your body?"

"He has to say that, you dingbat! The flowers were because you cried when you didn't celebrate your 25th wedding anniversary! If he were married to a perky breasted, warm, quivering-thighed twenty-year-old—he would have something to celebrate!

But look at yourself. Gray hair, overweight, you don't even laugh at his jokes any more. You don't treat him with respect. What's to feel romantic?"

"You're right."

"I'm always right. So give him up. Live in some small garret, downtown. Lie in bed all day. Wear dirty socks and panties that smell of herring; soft-bellied and dying on an off-shore fishing trawler, and in the immortal words of Frank Sinatra you can sing, *I did it—My Waaayy!*"

"No, that's not me. I'm bright. I'm fun. I look great. I have great sex. I love my man!"

"So you're going to 'Eat Him' tonight?"

"If I choose to I will, but it'll be my choice not yours."

VISION QUEST

"So tell me, oh stupid one, how was it when we first met?"

"I am on a vision quest, alone in a forest, sitting on a blanket surrounded by prayer ties."

"And what, oh wise and wondrous one, are prayer ties?"

"One inch bags of tobacco tied together with waxed string and prayers."

"And who is leading this so-called vision quest?"

"White Claw."

"Ah yes. The Native American woman with hair like a drowned cat and a body like cold pizza..."

"She warns me not to step outside the ties, not even for a pee, which is okay, because I had fasted for seven days."

"Beat me if I'm wrong, but do the words, *Anglo-Saxon white woman* and *vision quest* smack of oxymoron?"

"Turtle Island, *that's what Native Americans call it*, has welcomed me with a warm spirit, and I have opened my heart."

"Hallmark could use someone like you."

"Are you going to interrupt like this all the time?"

"Please continue, just keep it lively *dummkopf!*"

"I see tall, knobby kneed saplings, gnarled, loose skinned old trunks and baby green seedlings swaddled in a nursery of fallen logs."

"I envision you in a dark basement, quaffing tea and knocking out tear-jerkers by the meter."

"I'm painting the background."

"Don't."

"As the half light steels in, gray shapes swim in the air like pond life and I doze off. Some time later, I wake up sucking in great gasping lungs of freezing night air. Something has disturbed my sleep, but all I can see are ghostly paths of moonlight."

"Don't get flowery on me again," warns the dark side.

31

The woman ignores the voice. "Straight ahead is a tight-limbed tree with black clinging bark. It is unnaturally still, like a stealth bomber type insect."

"A Praying Mantis perhaps?" sniggers the dark side.

"Halfway up the trunk I notice a dark hollow the size of a farmer's hand."

"I like it there; dank and smelly like the armpit of a senile oak tree." The dark side takes a deep breath as it remembers the place.

"Something wills me to look."

"That's me, you idiot!"

"I see half a face. The left side is missing, but the right side stares directly at me from one unblinking eye."

"What about my smell? Aaahhh! Like the aroma of a bloated buffalo corpse floating mid-stream on a hot, paltry day."

"It is scary." The woman ignores the histrionics. "But at the same time, I know I have nothing to fear."

"That's what you think!"

"Grotesque creatures come at me from all sides, like Halloween masks in a toy store!"

"I do a good job, don't I?"

"Then I come face to face with a tall skeleton-figure cloaked in black." The woman gives an involuntary shudder. "I feel the marrow in my bones petrify."

"It is Death!"

"I know I have to confront it so I face it square on, and as I do, the chill in my heart slowly melts and my blood flows warm again."

"How long do you stare at it?"

"I have no idea. Slowly, my consciousness brings me back to the blanket."

"Then what?"

"You know what."

"Tell me."

"I get sexy feelings."

"It's more than sexy dear."

"Okay! I get so hot, I remember thinking that if I stick my butt into a bath of ice cold water, I could bring it to boiling point in an instant. The thought makes me laugh."

"You laugh far too much."

"So there I am. My fanny all fired up, and I can't stop laughing."

"Masturbation perhaps?"

"It's too cosmic for that ... I could light up a nuclear reactor plant!"

"What do you do, have a great roaring fuck with the universe?"

"I fall asleep with a smile on my ass!"

"And that's it? No bears or snakes with wondrous messages?"

"No."

"What about your husband?"

"He's beat, but he's having a great time. He and five sun dancers are keeping the fire going day and night, and on the last night, they invite him to drum in the sweat lodge."

"What's the big deal in that?" The dark side sounds peevish.

"They pray for guidance. Earlier in the month, one of the sun dancers had taken his great grandfather's headdress out of the country for a ceremony. It was made of eagle feathers, and when he brought it back through customs, they confiscated it!"

The dark side sees why immediately, "Because it's illegal to have feathers from an endangered species. Dumb twat!"

"But the eagle had given its feathers long before the law had been passed! It was his heritage, and a red-taped, dick-headed, customs official decided to impound it!"

"You humans do a good job of screwing things up."

"Yep!"

"So let me get this right! You get in touch with me, then you ignore me for two years?"

"I tell White Claw about you afterwards; she draws strange symbols over my head and tells me to forget you."

"So where do we go from here?"

"We could be friends."

"Lady. No one makes friends with the dark side."

"Why not?"

"You know that evil thought you had about slamming a baby to the ground and its head explodes."

"It wasn't my thought, so I let it go." The woman remembers the thought. She would never want to even contemplate such a thing. Is she completely mad?

"And what about when you're in a public place and you have the thought to scream or do something outrageous?"

"I don't create any of these thoughts, they don't belong to me. Thoughts come from the collective unconscious, like radio waves; we can tune into them or not. Some are like thought bombs; heat seeking missiles looking for a red hot emotional mind to explode in. Sure they come into my mind, but I identify them, and then detach myself from them. Eventually, they won't even bother coming into my mind."

"What's to stop me taking control and making you ignite these thoughts into action?"

"As a priest, my duty is to help heal the hurts of all sentient beings ... including you."

"And how, oh wuss bag of the first order, can you do that?"

"Meditation and detachment. Meditation strengthens my mind so that I can become detached from emotions."

"Become indifferent to life you mean?"

"No. Detachment does not mean indifference. For me, it means I am able to focus my energy in certain areas. I don't have to be mindless, or caught up in my emotions. Meditation brings peace and helps send peaceful thoughts to others."

"If you think you can bring peace to me, you're out of your mind."

"I don't want to be pushy. I'm simply here to support you."

"Lady, I do not need your help. I enjoy dark. Don't try to change me."

"I won't. Because of you, I made a conscious choice to grow toward the light, like a plant."

"You hate me don't you?"

"No," says the woman almost believing herself.

"Even though I nourish your head with hideous thoughts?"

"In mystical terms there is no dark side, no devil."

"So what am I?"

"You keep me from going over the top. You function to pull me back into reality. You're like a prison, you confine me and give me boundaries so that I can readjust myself."

"Lucifer! Why don't you just get off your high horse and come play in the shit with me!"

"It's funny you should say that. Yesterday I saw a beautiful, black and yellow butterfly in the back yard. It was like a petal floating on a light breeze. It landed on the lawn and stayed there for ages. Finally, I crept closer—I could hardly believe my eyes!"

"Don't tell me, it spoke to you in butterfly-ese."

"It was eating one of Millie's dog turds!"

"Butterflies have to eat."

"But here was this delicate creature, eating dog shit!"

"So what? Roses grow in horse shit and then people smell them!"

"So mystically, light things can feed off dark things and gain strength, like a butterfly."

"You said that mystically there is no dark or light."

"At this moment in time, I still perceive you as dark, but I don't have to be afraid of you any more, in fact, you may even help me become stronger."

"Never!"

"NEVER say never!!"

"It's very childish to want the last word, you know."

The woman wakes up the next morning after a dream about someone tattooing a baby's head. Was she the baby? Was it some kind of rebirth? She feels depressed, but makes the choice not to dial her mood up. Instead of going for her morning run she falls asleep. When she wakes, she picks up a book by Arnold Mindell, *The Shaman's Body* and starts to read a chapter about death and sorcery. The ideas are wonderful, but instead of feeling empowered, she looks around for a victim. Her husband is lying fast asleep beside her.

"Do you know that we all have dreaming bodies?"

"Wha's that?" The man splutters from the depths of a dream in which he has won the lottery and is flying his own plane to a tropical location where beautiful women are lined up with their bottoms in the air.

"Our dreaming bodies represent the person behind the words, the real us, the one we rarely show."

"Oh." Conversations like this upset him first thing in the morning, He tries silence.

"I think you and I are in different dreams," she continues to prod.

Silence.

"You want money and security, and I want spirituality."

"I don't think we're that much different," says the man, finally hooked. "I'm spiritual too. In fact I'm probably more spiritual than you are."

The woman remembers him coming home from a workshop led by D.E. Harding, author of *Head off Stress*. He told her about an exercise he did with a partner. Each stuck their face into one end of a twelve inch hollow tube with air holes punched in. Her husband said, that as he stared into his partner's face, he felt like he was looking out from space. As if he didn't exist.

Harding said to the group, "Drop your belief and imagination, and tell me how many faces are in the tube? Are you face-to-face, or face-to-space? Take in the human features of the face opposite, the contours, the shapes and compare these with your own lack of human features. Take in the coloring of the face, its various textures, its complexity, and compare these with your own colorlessness, your freedom from all blemishes."

Her husband said he experienced a complete lack of 'self' as if he had no face. "When I realized I was just space, I felt total harmony with the other person, as if we were both one! The woman at the other end of the tube actually started to cry. Tears rolled down her face."

"How old was she?"

"Late fifties," he answers.

"Unbelievable!" interjects the dark side, "Your man tells you this wonderful experience and all you think about is her age. You sure are a loser."

"I don't like that word *loser*," says the woman.

"Loser, loser, loser!" repeats the dark side in a *school playground* voice that reminds her of damp bottom smells and sweaty hair.

The woman brings her mind back to the present moment, "Maybe you are more spiritual than me," she says to her husband. "But I have to initiate everything." She wails off a list of everything she has started, "Meditation, becoming a vegetarian, the medicine wheel in the garden." Steve is sure he has initiated some things, but since he can't remember he remains silent.

The woman changes tack. "When Bob came by yesterday and said he liked the house the way it is, you said, (her voice assumes a high whine) *'but you should see the architect's plans, we're going to change this, and move this, and make this bigger.'* Why couldn't you just say, 'yeah, it's a great home!'"

"Pride. Plus I feel too pathetic."

"Well you are pathetic." Her words are soaked up like chamois leather. She babbles other words as a cover up, "I suppose you expect me to say that you are not pathetic. But frankly, if you think you are pathetic, it's better to admit it."

The tension makes her groin hot. Sex flashes in and out of her mind immediately followed by the thought: too messy, too energetic. She rolls to the edge of the bed, puts her feet on the floor and pushes herself into a sitting position.

"What are you doing?"

"Getting up." She doesn't add *"dummkopf."*

The man gets up also and together they silently pull, tuck, pat and smooth the sheets until the bed looks as inviting as a sleep commercial.

After his daily ablutions which he refers to as his, *shit, shower and shave*, Steve walks to the kitchen and calls, "Do you want breakfast?"

"What can we have?" she answers.

He reads 'DAY THREE' off a diet sheet taped to the cupboard door. It's designed for overweight heart patients seven days before surgery. He wonders why they continue to make life so difficult. "Fat burning soup or vegetables," he says despondently.

They drink a glass of pristine clear designer water, and the woman lectures him on her ideas about spirituality until finally he says, *"I'm really tired of you preaching at me!"*

Her surprise registers as a faint, "Oh."

"Where's all the laughter and the fun?" His forehead crumples into his hairline forcing the tiny follicles to bristle.

She can't think where the fun has gone. Her face draws in upon itself leaving her skin sallow with green empty looking veins. She hears his voice, but cannot summon the energy to answer.

"That's because she is under my spell." But even her dark side can't penetrate the cave she has built. It is dark in there, but it is also peaceful. Not having to do or say anything is like an elixir of life.

Her husband speaks again, "Do you want more water?"

Still she cannot answer. She feels like the 99th ape when it realizes it is being left behind on the path of evolution.

"Shall I go?" The man throws a question at her silence. Eventually he says, "I'm going to the office." He walks out the house, gets into the car and drives off.

Immediately after he has gone, the woman feels life flow back into her body and she goes to her writing room. Even the four inch hole seems comforting. An hour later, she hears his feet along the corridor. The door opens.

"Here is the file you wanted."

She takes the file and feigns interest. She senses there is more.

"I couldn't get the computer to work."

"Oh?"

"I couldn't move the little thing off the date."

The thing he is referring to is the cursor. "Why don't you take a computer class?"

"Then I would have to do everything..."

"No. It's a question of you catching up with the 20th century before it ends."

The conversation continues its downward spiral. "I don't know how to love you anymore," he says.

She hears this with panic, but refuses to let it show. "Then I should leave, go back to England."

"But do it this time. Don't just talk about it!" The man closes the door firmly behind him.

The dark side interrupts. "He really is fed up with your nastiness. You make him feel stupid!"

"I like to be nasty sometimes."

"So leave him."

"I don't want to."

"Yes you do. You wonder what it would be like on your own."

"I think of how lonely it would be."

"You would soon find someone else."

"I wouldn't want to. We're just going through a hard time that's all."

"It's been like this for 25 years. Get out while you can. He wants you to go. You make him feel worthless. You ain't doing him no good by staying!"

Minutes later the woman hears footsteps along the corridor. Her husband opens the door, "I didn't mean any of that. I don't know what I'm saying half the time."

"It's okay."

"No it's not. I've ruined your life as well as my own."

"I'm the one in charge of my life. It's got nothing to do with you," says the woman.

"That's bull-shit. I affect you. As soon as we react with other people—we have problems." He turns and walks out again.

"He's right. Listen to your husband."

"He's not right. It's up to me to be happy; no one else can do it for me."

"But if you are in a bad relationship ... then you will become unhappy."

"If I'm in a bad relationship then I can leave."

"So leave dumb-dumb!"

"I'm not in a bad relationship. I love him—he loves me. I wouldn't find anyone else I would rather spend my time with."

"So don't be a nasty cunt."

"For a dark side, you're not very subtle."

"I'm not in a personality contest you numb nut!"

The woman hears the front door slam. Outside the window, thin, straggly bushes reach up from roadside grass colored: *Exhaust Brown 303*. A concrete telegraph pole stands idle with its wires in curlers. The antique glass distorts the lines of the train station parking lot into wavy worms. She pushes the sash up and calls to Steve in a lilting voice which she hopes sounds like a smile, "Are you coming back?"

"No, I'm going to keep on running!" His words are spoken with querulous hope; unsure of the truce flag.

"Bless your life with every step of the way."

"What life?" His voice holds a remnant of hope.

"The life you have. All the wonderful things in it. Me, you, our children, everything."

"I've made such a mess of it."

"No you haven't. I love you."

He waves and the woman waves back. She feels horny again.

"That's because of your emotions."

"What?"

"You were too angry to say you wanted to make love. But imagine if you had?"

"We would have stopped arguing."

"And that wouldn't do, would it?" sniggers the dark side.

"Yes it would."

"Next time you argue and feel horny, tell him."

"It seems dirty, rude."

"Would you rather act dirty, or have an argument?"

"Okay, I'll do it."

"But not for me. Do it for yourself. Either way you should give in to your sex drive more often. You would have more fun that way."

"If I give in to sexual thoughts when I am angry, I may have to keep having arguments to have sex. That's why soldiers rape after battles. I don't want to be like that."

"Suit yourself."

"Thanks, I will. I'll make love to my husband tonight, and it will be out of love and passion."

"Don't forget to eat him ... you still haven't done that have you?"

"Actually I have!" She turns off the computer and goes downstairs.

INNER WORLDS

"She said there are going to be two bullets used, I don't know what to do!" Peter hands her a cup of coffee. "She goes through my pockets looking for phone numbers and names. She wants me to take a polygraph test!"

Just then, the kitchen door opens and in walks Sheila. Usually an attractive woman, her skin has the texture of home-made paper, and her roots need a touch up. She slams down a yellow Post-it on the kitchen table, "I want her name and phone number!"

"Sheila, I don't have a name," says Peter. His voice sounds like an assistant funeral director trying to learn the correct tonality to use.

"I want her name and I want it now!"

The woman strokes the yellow edges of a trembling fern whose task is to decorate the table. She wonders how to leave without being noticed. The door opens again and in walk two of the couple's four children, Ben, and Jane. Sheila continues to stab at the Post-it, "Give me her name!"

"Let's go see the flowers in your garden." The woman takes hold of Jane's hand and leads her outside. Ben the older of the two, stays with his parents.

"Who painted your toe nails?" The four-year-old toes are dabbed with bright pink polish like a tiny row of wieners.

"My big sister!"

"Did you go swimming in the lake?"

The little girl shakes her head, and black hair swishes up like midnight raindrops.

"Why not? You love to swim."

She looks at her toes and whispers, "I didn't want the seaweed to take the color off."

"It wouldn't do that. Nail polish is very strong." But the little girl already knows that grownups lie. They sit surrounded by the silence of plant life. Only the wind has the energy to whisper.

After a while, Peter comes out carrying a large trash bag which he throws in the garbage. As he walks over to them, his face crumples like a handkerchief tossed in the laundry, he covers it with his hands. "I can't stand going through another week-end like this." The woman goes to him, he is a small fat man and as she folds her arms around his shaking body, she feels like a mother seal wrapping her baby against the cold sea. Wet tears fall strangely against her cheek. "She's off the wall. I don't know what to do," says Peter.

The woman thinks for a moment. "Peter, are you having an affair?"

"No!" He is adamant.

"Are you telling me the truth?" She has to be sure.

"As God is my witness I am not having, nor ever have had, an affair." He looks up to the heavens as if God is standing with gavel in hand.

"You are about as useful as a garlic press at a Bible meeting." The dark side loves sardonic humor—the woman ignores it.

Ben walks out just then, "Mom says for you to take us to her sister's house; here are the keys." He throws the keys to his dad, and they stand in a small huddle wondering what to do next.

As a silence filler, the woman says, "Would you like me to talk to Sheila?" She is surprised by the depth of his response.

"Would you, please." Galvanized into action Peter piles the kids into the car and drives off. When the tail lights disappear the woman enters the house.

Sheila is sitting at her table slowly turning the well thumbed pages of her husband's day timer and carefully scrutinizing each name and phone number. "Did you see Peter on the freeway last Wednesday?" Sheila asks.

The woman's mind furiously races through its filing cabinets but draws a blank. "I don't think…"

"It was about eight or nine in the morning."

"Ah yes! I was driving downtown, and recognized his car in front. I pulled up alongside and waved." It had zero importance in her life, but Peter must be using it as proof of his whereabouts.

"He's really hurt me."

"What's he done?"

"He's having an affair ... I just don't know who with! He doesn't even sound like Peter anymore. He's using someone else's words."

"He meets a lot of people, we all pick up different phrases."

"He told me he once had an affair with an older woman— before we were married," Sheila quickly adds. "I think she called yesterday."

"How old will the woman be now?" asks the woman.

"Fifty-five, maybe sixty."

"Sheila, there's no way. I mean..." The woman feels the liberation of a confession well up, "I went with a forty-two-year-old man when I was nineteen, my God he probably uses a walker now, ugh!" She shakes her head at the thought of old flesh pressing against hers. Wrinkles, smelling of trapped cologne.

The confession passes over Sheila's head. "He won't give me her last name!"

"Why do you want it?"

"To get her social security number and find out if she's been to Chicago recently."

"If I were Peter I wouldn't give you her name; what if you called her husband? You could ruin a whole marriage."

"I won't call her husband. I just need her social security number. Anyway if he were innocent he would take a polygraph test."

"If he had one and proved he was telling the truth, would you believe him then?"

"Probably not! What I really want is a private detective."

The woman feels the customary shiver down her neck. The one thing she doesn't need right now is her dark side. "You nearly did that once, didn't you?" says the dark side.

"I was jealous, but I never actually hired one."

"Now do you see what jealousy does to a person?"

"It curls itself round the mind until it consumes it," thinks the woman.

"It's one of my greatest weapons. It ranks up there with greed. I'd give it a good eight or nine points."

"Sheila." The woman opens her heart to speak. "I know that Peter is not having an affair."

Sheila's eyes focus on her like steel pointed needles, "How do you know?"

"I just do." The woman has no idea how she knows, she simply feels it to be true. "Peter is not having an affair, and he has never had an affair. I just know it."

For a moment Sheila looks almost sane. "Are you sure?"

"As sure as I'm standing here in front of you. Peter is a sweet man. Do you love him?"

"Yes."

"Does he love you?"

A slight hesitation, "Yes. I think so."

"Sheila, the jealousy is within *you!* It has nothing to do with Peter."

"Part of me knows that. I even went to a psychiatrist and he said I have a lot of anger inside. I threw a tray of cookies at Peter yesterday." Sheila looks around her house as if it is about to be put on a trailer and towed away.

"Have you always been jealous of Peter?"

"I think so. He had lots of girlfriends before we met. I never really trusted him."

This picture of Peter does not correspond with what the woman knows of him: a quiet family man who loves his children and wants an uncomplicated life.

"Would you like a healing?"

Sheila looks at her as if she holds the answer. "Yes, I think I would."

"We could have my husband and Peter there too if you like."

"Yes that would be good."

"Call me when you're ready." Sheila walks the woman to the door.

Later that evening the phone rings. "Hi, it's Sheila. Thanks for the talk. I would like to have that healing."

"When would you like it?"

"Tonight?"

The woman's heart sinks like a stone. Tonight is the one night she cannot do it. She has a meditation class arriving in ten minutes. "I can't tonight, what about tomorrow?"

The dark side jumps in, "Call yourself a healer? The woman is desperate, she needs help, you said you would give it!"

"I can't right now."

"What if the emergency room said that to a bleeding patient?"
"I'm not a doctor."
"You set yourself up as a healer," smirks the dark side.
"I don't set myself up as anything. Besides, healing doesn't necessarily mean getting physically better. It's more a healing of the soul."
"How do you know when a soul is better?"
"When the person understands why they feel the pain, when they have awareness of what caused it and why it manifested."
"Sounds like fluff to me. But go ahead. Sheila is asking for help and you won't give it."
"I asked Sheila many times to come to meditation, it may have helped her. Now it's like putting a band-aid on a severed artery. She needs more help than I can give." The woman goes back to her phone conversation with Sheila. "Tomorrow it is then." They both put down the phone.
"I don't understand," begins the woman. "It is so difficult to obtain this humanoid form, and our life is so uncertain and brief, yet we continually fritter it away."
"Are you saying that Sheila is frittering her life away?" asks the dark side.
"Yes and no," replies the woman. "If she could reach out to her children, her husband, beyond her own limitations she may grow stronger."
"Poppycock," says the dark side. "She needs a pill to restore the chemical imbalances in her brain!"
"Maybe," says the woman. "But if she could see beyond what she thinks she sees, if she could understand the Reality."
"Reality, shmality!" says the dark side. "Give her a pill and she'll be fine."
"If she could learn how to release those chemicals within herself," persists the woman, "she would be better!"
"Dial the pharmacy in her head you mean?" snorts the dark side.
"Exercise, meditate, find ways to release the pent-up anger." Says the woman quietly. "That's what I mean."
"Sheila prefers a pill she can see!" says the dark side. "A pill is most efficacious in the situation."

"You're right," says the woman, remembering her own Hormone Replacement Therapy and what her doctor said after the hysterectomy.

"You need to take these pills or your vagina will shrivel like a walnut!" The doctor made his hand into a fist. "And it will be impossible to make love!" Her husband, who was in on the discussion looked aghast at this last statement.

"Just keep taking the pills," said the doctor, "and you'll be fine!"

GUILT OF CHOICE

"The problem is that you have no tradition." The monotone voice of her dark side is like a damp drip in a cold cellar; she looks at the bedside clock ... it is precisely 2:45AM. "You don't even have a regular job!" persists the dark side.

Before bed, the woman had watched the Queen of England have her portrait painted. Swathed in velvet pinned with medals she told her subjects, "I know what I'll be doing next month, next year and even the year after that. I think it's good for one ... then one knows what to expect from day to day ... it's tradition. And of course training is very important also ... if one is well trained, one can accomplish anything!" The Queen set her features into the expressionless portrait that stares at her subjects from a variety of stamps, coinage and pound notes.

"See! Training and Tradition. Neither of which you have," the dark side jumps in.

The woman responds, saying, "I write. That takes discipline."

"Writers, my dear dufus, have set times when they fiddle at the keyboard! You on the other hand, are at the whim of creatures like me."

"As long as one gets one's job done." The woman mimics the Queen's impersonal style of speech.

"Imagine if the Queen said that, 'Duke dear, I've decided not to launch the *Queen Mary* today, tell them to keep it in dry dock until I feel in a better mood.'"

"The Queen has at least three private secretaries, and God knows how many Ladies in Waiting ... she doesn't have the problems of everyday folk."

"She could have chosen to be a big fat slob like some of her ancestors."

"Why are you sticking up for the Queen of England?"

"I'm simply using her as a point of reference. She's a strong woman whose life is steeped in tradition, family and training.

47

You are a weak woman whose life is drowning in self-indul-
gence and uselessness."
    "She's lucky to be trained as Queen. No one ever taught me to
be anything. I've had to learn everything myself."
    "Aaaawww ... poor little victim!"
    "That's how I feel sometimes."
    "You have no mommy and not much of a daddy."
    The woman thought she had gotten over her father. But last
night she had composed a letter: *Dear dad, I'm writing to tell
you that you haven't been much of a dad to me. You never write,
you never phone, you never visit. You haven't bothered with my
children. You never acknowledge their birthdays. You never buy
them gifts. You don't even know they've graduated from college.
You wouldn't send me money when I needed it. I never even feel
like I have a dad! Dads are supposed to love their daughters ...
have a soft spot for them. What makes you so indifferent?*
    "Not a very nice letter, is it? Why don't you send it to him?
At his age, It will probably make him *pop his clogs.*"
    "That's just it. I haven't been a great daughter, but I do visit
him when I'm in England."
    "You didn't the last time."
    "I couldn't squeeze it in."
    "Bullshit."
    "It's just not worth it. He only wants me to visit for a couple
of hours. It takes two hours to get to his place ... we talk for a
bit ... they feed me..."
    "Your stepmother feeds you."
    "It's the least she can do. Her grandson is all they care about.
My dad made this huge model farm for him; it's in their front
room and when he visits, which is every day, he plays with it."
    "Your stepmother's daughter lives across the road from them.
You moved to America!"
    "Steve's mom visits us from the north of England. She writes
to my children. She cares."
    "Which proves we're all different. If you want to be a great
daughter, you can be. It doesn't matter whether your dad
deserves it or not. You can write, visit, send photographs of the
children—keep him up to date. You just never bothered."
    "Because he never bothered!"

"That's like an abused child continuing the tradition. He's not a great dad, so you won't be a great daughter. Break the mold. Grow up!"

"Okay, I'll make a big effort, I'll write him a nice letter today, and put in some photos."

"And I'll eat my butt! And what about the tradition you don't have?"

"It sucks. I can't summon any enthusiasm for Christmas because there's no family here to share it with."

"You have two children ... what more could you want?"

"I want a tradition that already exists ... so I can keep it going. It's hard to start traditions."

"Stop moaning and live your life."

"I wake up in the morning with ugly thoughts about my life and what's missing."

"I do a great job don't I? I play around in your head when you are dreaming, and you wake up feeling like dog poop."

"It's very tiring."

"So fight me."

"I don't want to fight."

"So live with it."

"Somehow I have to find a way of dealing with you so that you don't take my energy ... to ignore you maybe? You see I really do have a great life."

"Concentrate on what's bad; it's much better to be a victim than a winner. Winning is too hard for a weakling like you."

"I guess I'm like a battery with negative and positive. Neither one is good or bad, but for the battery to function, the two forces have to work together."

"You will never succeed."

"I don't want to deny my dark side, I just don't want it taking over."

"But I do take over. Every morning when you wake up feeling bad, that's me. My power and influence are very strong. Remember what Queenie said about training, and how important it is. Well sweetie, you have no training, you are as useless as a bald tree to a leaf cutting ant."

"I'm self-taught."

"But there's no one to give you feedback."

"I get feedback from the people in my life. I have friends ... so I must be okay at something."

"And you lose friends, so you must be bad at something."

"Hey, the Queen's family isn't all that great. Divorce ... bulimia ... mistresses... lovers. Imagine all the deceit and lying that goes on. I'm not like that."

"You've been bulimic."

"Once or twice I have stuck my finger down my throat after a serious binge on ice cream ... but it's more because I felt so full that I thought my stomach would burst."

"That's bulimia."

"It's not a regular thing; once or twice a year, not every week."

"You stood in the shower and vomited into the bath tub and little bits of carrot splattered against the curtain. You're sick in the head. Besides, your son was bulimic, so don't be throwing stones at Queenie's glass palace."

"My son wanted to keep within his wrestling weight—I was very upset when I found out."

"Balls! He was getting over a serious emotional trauma. Unless you don't count getting his girlfriend pregnant and having an abortion as serious!"

"She wasn't even out of high school. She was too young to look after a baby."

"You could have adopted, or helped raise it."

"In retrospect I could have done that. But at the time, she didn't want it. We talked it over with them."

"You helped murder your own grandchild."

"I admit, I haven't been a great mother. It's because mine died when I was young. I didn't have a role model to follow."

"There are plenty of good mothers who don't have role models; they've done okay."

"I need to forgive myself."

"Why bother? You're a lousy mother."

"I would forgive anyone else."

The fan above the woman's head cools the air. Five hundred people have already died in Chicago's hot summer. Does anybody feel guilty about that? Old people with electricity cut off; so hot they can only lie in bed and stare at walls. The woman wonders if they died in pools of sweat, or did their wrinkled bodies become so dehydrated their skin turned to parchment? She is strangely removed from the tragedy. Much easier to feed personal guilt.

"I admit I haven't been a great mother. But given the tools and the training, I did the best I could."

"A good cop out."

"What am I supposed to do, beat myself to death? Walk into the post office and kill a few postal workers? I have to forgive myself, then I can do a better job."

"How, when you've built your life on a series of lousy jobs?"

"Because I learn. Each time I do something wrong, I learn another way of how not to do it."

"It sounds good, but you keep on doing a lousy job."

"Jesus died on the cross to forgive my sins."

"Whoa! Where did that come from? And you, not even a Christian?"

"It's symbolic. My old self has to die so my new self can be reborn."

"So you believe in abortion?"

"A friend told me about an abortion she had years ago; she was sixteen when her mom took her by train to the city, to a woman who did illegal abortions. There was no anesthetic, just dirty surroundings and an unqualified nurse who wanted her in and out as quickly as possible. She went back on the train with her stomach in cramps and lost the fetus somewhere between stations. As long as we have unwanted pregnancies, we will find ways to get rid of them. I would rather it be in a lawful and hygienic way."

"I thought being a light-minded person you wouldn't want to kill lives!"

"I don't. But until we make motherhood a proud and wonderful thing for every woman, including single, teenage girls, until we help people raise kids properly, we need the right to choose."

"Why didn't you make sure your son used a condom?"

"I thought he did."

"If women were on the pill, there wouldn't be a problem."

"So why don't they hand out free pills? In France contraceptives are free. Besides, why should it always be the woman's responsibility?" says the woman.

"I bet there are still French women who won't take it."

"It's called freedom to choose."

"You allowed both your children to have sex in the house. I think it's great personally, but it doesn't quite fit the picture of a swami priest."

"I wasn't a priest then. I didn't know any better."

"You have an answer for everything, don't you."

"Okay, okay. I'm guilty of being a lousy parent. I'm making amends for it now."

"Too late. The damage is done."

"No, no, no! To say the damage is done, is to say that my children are damaged."

"Well they are."

"They are wonderful human beings. They are sensitive, loving, caring people. I couldn't wish for better children. If they have been damaged in any way, they have turned it into wisdom, because they both have an inner knowing."

"Very convenient if you ask me."

The woman feels as if all the air in the room has been sucked out, her lungs, like black tubes filled with tar, she cannot breathe.

At that moment, her husband walks into the room in running shorts and t-shirt. She heard him making 'dressing' sounds earlier. He has fed the dog. Now he is standing behind her reading the computer screen. Annoyance flames through her like fire on rice paper. He puts his hand on her head and strokes her hair. It is like a fly crawling across her skin. "I'm off, bunky," he says. *Bunky* is one of her nicknames. *Rose-garden* is another.

The woman turns and says in a tight voice, "Right, off you go then!"

"Oh, okay." He tip toes out like the Pink Panther.

"It doesn't matter how much you meditate, or talk about being giving and loving—you still have an ugly, ugly, personality!"

"I know." The woman decides to go for a run too, the dark side rarely follows her outdoors.

THE BLOW JOB

It's the day of the AIDS results. Both her children go to the testing center in Waukegan, while the woman stays home and waits.

"Wimping out again!"

"They didn't want me to go."

"That's what happens after a lifetime of non-support."

"That's not true."

"Did you help them with homework? Teach them any discipline?"

"I admit I didn't do a good job in everything. I did show them lots of love though."

"You smacked them!"

"Only across the legs, besides, I didn't know any better."

"That's what murderers on death row say."

"In a way they're right. We all do the best we can. Sometimes our best seems very bad ... but it's still the best. Did you hear the story of the prostitute and the priest?"

"No, but I'm sure you will manage to screw it up."

"Every night after the prostitute had sold his body..."

"Very funny!" says the dark side. "Calling the prostitute male—most sardonic!"

"It is such a male world and so much writing assumes that prostitutes are women and priests are men that I want to make a point."

"Well don't, nobody cares."

"I bet lots of people reading this even think you are male!" says the woman chuckling to herself.

"Well I'm certainly not female!"

"You're certainly not male!" says the woman taking a deep breath. "So, the prostitute looked across at the priest's house and thought, 'How wonderful to be that priest, to have peaceful thoughts of God. To love others even though they have sinned.' Every night, the prostitute went to sleep thinking kind and loving thoughts about the priest. Every night after the priest had prayed, she looked across at the prostitute's house and thought, 'How terrible to be that prostitute, to live a life of sin. To sell your body and to be surrounded by wicked, lustful people.' Every night the priest went to sleep thinking about all the lustful, evil temptations of the flesh. Eventually, they both die, but there is only one place in heaven and God has to choose. Who got chosen?"

"Surprise me," yawns the dark side.

"The prostitute. Because even though he had sold his body, his mind was centered on the loving thoughts of the priest. While the priest, even though she spent all her time praying, dwelled on sin."

"These stupid little stories make me want to vomit. The reality is, that the prostitute defiled her body and the priest strengthened his mind." The dark side is intent on keeping to the female stereotype of a prostitute.

"No, while the prostitute was thinking love, the priest was thinking sin. The reality is that we become what we most think about."

"I can't be bothered to argue. Where were we?"

"The AIDS center in Waukegan. Did you know it only uses numbers ... there are no names, addresses, social security numbers, or anything that can link the AIDS test to a person? Perfect anonymity. And after the results, each person has a half-hour debriefing session."

One hour later her daughter's car swings into the driveway. The woman watches, her heart like a torpedoed submarine. "It's..." For a moment Silva is going to pretend the worst, but when she sees her mother's shrunken face she smiles, "It's okay Momma, it's negative."

The woman wraps her arms around her daughter and squeezes tightly. All she can say is, "Thank God."

"God shmod." The dark side has to comment. "She's lucky that's all." The woman ignores the voice; this is too important a celebration to get infected.

"Let's get some lunch, I'll call dad."

At the restaurant there is surprisingly little to say. A negative result does not have as much charge as a positive one. "But you have to give your stupid little lecture!" says the dark side sardonically.

"All I said was, *be careful next time.*"

"The voice of gloom and doom. They give them a talk at the test center about AIDS, how it's passed along, and how to prevent it."

"I have a right to add my bit, I'm a parent."

"That's debatable."

"It's strange how quickly everything gets back to normal. The horror is forgotten and life's little problems take over. It's like a beetle stuck on its back, kicking and struggling. Once it's flipped over it does exactly the same thing that got it stuck in the first place."

"Beetles don't have big brains."

"Neither do humans when it comes to repeating bad habits."

"Aha ... so you're learning that humans are stupid. Now you can see how easy it is to be a dark side. All I have to do is point out the stupid stuff and build up the guilt. By the way, have you eaten your man yet?"

"Yes, late Friday afternoon we were at the office and no one else was there. I switched the computers off and heard Steve lock the front door."

"So you knew that sex was about to rear its ugly head."

"He coughs and I look up," continues the woman, envisioning the moment.

"Why are you switching to present tense?"

"It's more interesting. Anyhow stop interrupting me." The woman recalls where she was at in the story, "Steve pokes his penis round the doorway like an overstuffed Chinese egg roll."

"It reminds you of food?"

"I put on my best Mae West accent, 'Over here big boy,' and he shuffles in."

"It's hard to walk with my pants round my ankles," laughs Steve. "Are you ready for some Polish sausage?"

"He's not very romantic, is he?"

"He's very funny. We laugh a lot when we have sex."

I say, "I want to give you a blow job."

He says, "Aw no. You don't have to for me."

"I want to."

"Are you sure?"

"Absolutely. Come here," I say. "And I put my mouth around his penis and suck."

"When I start to come," he turns his head down toward me, "you have to suck really hard." The three worry-creases on his brow etch deeper, and his face is hot and red, like he's just come off a sunbed.

I nod my head, determined to swallow.

"Hold my balls." The husband gives stage directions as if he's performing a dress rehearsal. "HOLD ON ... IT'S HERE."

The woman's cheekbones suck into her skull, like she's drawing water from a 200-foot well.

"Agghhh." The man's face fractures like a Picasso painting. She sucks even harder.

"No, no, no, stop, stop, STOP!" He pulls himself away. Sperm ejects through the air like a hyperactive water pistol with Attention Deficit Disorder.

"What's the matter? What did I do wrong?"

"Ahhaha." The man is bent over like a broken boomerang. "I think my cock is going to explode."

"But you told me to suck really hard."

"I didn't know how hard you could suck."

"I was all ready to swallow." The woman is disappointed.

The dark side has to have its voice. "You should be used to not completing things."

"It's depressing, especially when I hear other women say how much they enjoy it. A wife told me just the other day that she only has to put her mouth into an O shape and her husband practically comes on the spot."

The following Thursday the woman wakes early. She pushes up on her elbow to see the clock emblazon 4:05AM in red, square letters. With all the stealth of a cat burglar dressed in hot pink, she inches her fingers across the bed space until they touch her husband's warm body. His pubic hair is springy, like sphagnum moss. She reaches for his penis. It rests in her hand like the soft inside of a French loaf.

The man turns fully on his back and stretches his legs with a shudder. "Wha'ya doin?" He mumbles. "I'll have to go for a pee now!" He gets up, and drags his feet to the bathroom as if his legs are without knees.

The woman waits for his return.

"And what about the urine drops on the end?" The dark voice relentlessly seeks out unpleasant thoughts.

"I don't care. I'm going to do it."

"Why not wait until he's showered?"

"I said, I'm going to do it, and that's what I'm going to do."

"Be it on your own head then, pun intended."

Steve gets back into bed and lays on his back. The woman leans over and takes it into her mouth.

"You don't have to do this." The husband knows her fear of throwing up. "You even gag when the dentist puts his finger on your back molars."

The woman gently sucks and allows random thoughts to float through her mind like the moon cloaked leaves of a silver birch tree: *It's like a plumbing system and I'm clearing a pipe. I wonder how long it will take? Is he enjoying this? Am I doing it properly? How would a prostitute do it?*

"IT'S COMING!" The man shouts as if an express train is about to tear through their bedroom. She tastes salt. Feels her throat spasm. Hears Steve laugh. Swallows.

"Oh my God I did it!"

"That was the funniest thing."

"I actually gave you a blow job."

"I thought you were going to throw up."

"I could do it again any time."

"I don't really enjoy it, to be honest with you."

"That's not the point, I did it."

"Yes you did."

For once the dark side has nothing to say. The man and the woman fall back asleep. She feels like she has climbed Mount Everest and planted a pubic hair on top. In the early morning, she dreams of flying. High, sweeping and free.

How Dark Is Dark?

"Okay, entertain me!"

The woman and her husband are sitting in what she calls the lounge. It's Friday after a long week. "Do you ever have any **REALLY DARK** thoughts?" she asks.

He would rather watch a tortoise climb Sears Tower than have this kind of conversation, but he's been married long enough to know that he must answer. "Of course I do."

"Like what?" His silence prods her to continue. "I mean, does a thought ever enter your head like..." She dares to say it, "throwing a baby down on the ground?"

"Of course."

"It does?" She is shocked that her gentle hubby would entertain such a thought.

"I sometimes think of poking someone's eye out." He stabs at the air with his forefinger and hooks it round an imaginary eyeball.

"That's not the same as a baby."

"I could throw a child on the floor and stamp on its head until it looked like raspberry jam."

"Ugh!"

"Who hasn't thought of murdering someone, or eating human flesh? Cutting off a little piece of ass and tasting it."

This is not a thought the woman has had ... it makes hers seem less frightening. "So what stops us from doing these things?"

"I don't really know. Just a mechanism."

"So what happened to Sheila's mechanism?"

Sheila had not come for a healing. The day before, the woman had gone round and found her sifting through the garbage, heaping clumps of old food into an empty can of peas. "Peter is trying to poison us ... he put Cocaine in our food." Sheila walks on tiptoe and puts her perspiring face up close and whispers, "He's

a big time drug dealer… I've had him followed." Banana peel
and melon seeds spill onto the floor as Sheila shoves her arm to
the bottom of the garbage. "The whole house is bugged. They're
watching us. I think they have a contract out on me!"

Just then, the door opens and Chuck walks in. He is another of
Sheila's neighbors. "If you want to see something really grue-
some, go to Wellington Road. There's a man bleeding out there."
Chuck walks to the freezer, grabs a handful of ice, puts it in a
plastic bag and presses it to his right knuckle.

"He's a drug dealer," says Sheila. "My poor husband!" With
this she begins to cry. "We have to break him."

"I don't think he's on drugs," says the woman.

"Last night you guys…" Sheila puts her arms out to indicate
they should go into a huddle. "We had sex like you would never
believe—it must be the drugs!" The woman is torn between titil-
lation and not wanting to breathe the same air. "He was like a
wild boar." Sheila's eyes glaze over. "He was not like my
husband. It was … it was…" Her eyes search the room for
inspiration. "It was sultry." She stands back and rotates her hips
forward as if she is being screwed in a back alley.

"Sheila, if he wasn't married to you. I would give you a good
one!" Chuck smiles as if he has just delivered a compliment.

The woman takes small breaths through her nose and tries to
change the subject. "What about the man on the road?"

Chuck inspects his knuckles. "I was at a red light when this
jerk comes up behind me and honks his horn, but it's a *No Turn
On Red,* so I sit and wait for green. Then he brings his car real
close and nudges me forward, so I get out my car, walk to his
car, and shout through his window, 'If you don't want your nose
shoved through your brains you had better stay in your car!' But
he starts to get out, so I slam the door on his knees. Then I hit
him on the nose; I think I broke it!"

"I want my poor husband back." Sheila is now throwing all
the contents of the refrigerator into the garbage. "He's trying to
poison us, Chuck."

"I was in the Navy … I was a Seal. I was in Vietnam. I know
how to kill men!"

The woman wonders how she came to be in this place at this
particular time with these strange people.

"Sheila, next time you come round early in the morning to see my wife, you gotta call first." Chuck rests his hand on Sheila's shoulder. "I nearly shot you this morning. I thought you was an intruder!"

"Okay I'll call. But you're my neighbor, Chuck. You have to be there for me." Sheila dials her father's number. "Dad, you have to come and help me break Peter. We have to stop him going with his Mafia friends." Within the hour, her father, sister, aunt and mother arrive at the house. All weekend long people come and go, shuffling to and from hospitals and doctor's rooms. Sheila insists that both she and Peter are tested for drugs. They come back negative. Finally, Sheila is committed into Hospital from where she writes her husband, "I don't ever want to come home again ... everyone thinks I am a lunatic."

"Yes. I'm happy to say, another one under my thumb." Her dark side has enjoyed the whole spectacle.

"I've done that kind of stuff," says the woman. "I've thought my husband was having affairs when he wasn't and if I'd had the money, I'd have had him followed. One time I burned the car engine out by driving into London without any oil in it. I was so crazy I didn't even stop at a garage." The woman recollects the feeling of lunacy. "Maybe if Sheila could go within and look at her dark side, she wouldn't feel so bad. I mean, she's not alone with these kind of feelings!"

"No my dear child." Her dark side patronizes her. "Unless you are a doctor, or a loony tune like you, it is inadvisable. Look at you. You're supposed to be a priest and your thoughts are like craters full of sewage. You feed off other people's emotions; you could have gone to your own house and shut the door."

"Yes."

"You were excited by the drama."

"Yes."

"You're a bad person, a worse priest and a lousy neighbor."

"I'm human."

"That's no excuse."

"This earth plane is not perfect. If it were, I would not be here. I'm here to grow and learn. I make mistakes. And that's okay," says the woman.

"What about stealing from one of your close friends, is that human?" The dark side feeds on the stillness of the moment.

Her friend Kate had gone away for a few days and asked the woman to feed Edward her cat. On the table was a special meditation tape. The woman needed some new and different meditation music so when she saw the tape, it seemed the perfect opportunity. She could copy it without even having to ask.

"You knew it would upset her ... it was a special tape."

"I thought about asking."

"You knew she would say no."

"After I copied it, I put the tape back."

"Then the turds hit the turd-thrasher. At her next meditation, Kate put the tape in, and it was the wrong tape."

"I had replaced it with my own by mistake."

"You thought about lying."

"But I didn't. I came clean and told her everything."

"You waffled on about how you might be trying to steal her power. Do you really want to be like her?"

"No. I want to be like myself... I want to feel my own power."

"You want to suck people's power from them like a leech."

The woman realizes this is partly true. "Yes. Then everyone will listen to me and I will be like a guru."

"So come my little one, the next time you get caught out, lie! You could say, 'Kate, I don't know how it happened, but you have my tape and I have yours.' She would think spirit played tricks on you both."

"I don't want to lie."

"Look cunt-chops, now you've told the truth, what does she think of you?"

"That I am truthful?"

"No STUPIDO! She thinks you are a liar and a thief."

"But I came clean."

"About the fact that you lie and steal, and want to take her power. Trust me, next time, lie!"

In a way the woman almost believes her dark side.

"You are right to believe me. Remember last meditation, Steve admitted he was a liar, and what happened? Bonnie said, 'Yes I can see it in your eyes.' Then Claire said, 'So I can't believe anything you say?'"

The woman remembers how quickly the group wanted to believe the worst of Steve rather than recognize the truthfulness of his confession.

"Exactly! All he did was brand himself a liar! Coming clean does not wipe the slate clean, it just ingrains it more!"

The woman says, "It's like a well, there has to be dirty water while it's being scrubbed clean."

"So?"

"Eventually, the well will run clean. Besides, it takes energy to lie. I have to remember the truth and the lie. Then I have to make up a whole lot of lies to cover up the truth. It's a big mess."

"But it's a mess only you know about. Why show everyone the dirty laundry that's inside your head?"

"Because it cleans me out. It makes way for new and more interesting thoughts."

"Oh shove it cheese-ball. I'm sick and tired of your hokey-pokey spiritual sayings. Lie, cheat, swear, do drugs, live and let live. Have some fun for Devil's sake."

"I'd rather have fun for my own sake."

Silva's boyfriend Jordan and friend Shanda all come for dinner that evening. They choose an African recipe, and go to the shops to buy ingredients. The woman is setting the table when the husband says, "Have we got bread?"

"No!" replies the woman.

"What about butter?"

"I didn't think about it."

"How can you think about dinner without bread and butter?"

"We have rice."

"But the kids want bread."

"They won't mind."

"Yes they will."

"If you want bread, go to the shops and get some," she says.

"I don't want bread. It's for the kids."

"Of course he wants the bread. Just get it, you skivvy." Even the dark side wearies of these tit-for-tat arguments.

The woman also feels it's not worth arguing the point. That morning, the husband spent half-an-hour on the phone with an IRS lady trying to get an extension on back taxes they have just found out about. She would rather go for bread than have that job. Besides, he got the extension, which was just as well, because now they do not have to concern themselves about the registered letter telling them that the IRS will put a lien on the house ... at least not for the time being.

The woman meets up with the three young adults at the checkout counter for *Under Ten Items*. She asks Jordan in an urgent voice, "Can you get me some, *I Can't Believe It's Not Butter*, butter?"

He looks at her as if she has asked him to climb a coconut tree, "Wha...?" She can see his mind whirring like a dervish. "Is it in a tub or..."

She thinks, Oh God save me from idiots, "It's in blocks."

His hands make square shapes as if he is playing charades. "Like this?" he says.

Silva interrupts, "It's in sticks, Jordan!"

But he hasn't finished playing the idiot quite, "Where...?"

The woman looks up the aisles to where it says, Dairy Products, "It's the third one along." She does not add, "dumb, dumb!"

Running to the bread isle, she squeezes two French sticks and like a well-drilled bread connoisseur, selects the softest and runs back to the *Under Ten Items* checkout. Furtively counting and re-counting, she realizes her bread brings the total items to twelve. The man behind her in line holds his solitary bottle of wine as if he should win the 'minimalist' shopper award.

Jordan saunters from the cereal aisle, empty handed! "I couldn't find..." Jumping on his lame excuse, the woman assumes a running Groucho Marx walk, pushing aside a laughing couple as if they are in breach of shopping etiquette, and returns to the check-out with yet another item. The wine man puffs up his chest, then breathes out quietly. On second thought, he thinks this woman might be the type to carry a shotgun in her shopping basket! He remains quiet.

Back home, in the kitchen they peel, chop and slice. It feels like a sixties commune. During dinner, silly things pop out of her mouth as if she is a teenager, youthful, fresh and alive. Her children and she are really close these days ... almost like strangers who realize they have a lot in common. Oh the fun of life ... even the pain in her left side is getting better, perhaps she doesn't have cancer after all.

"Aha! so you're still worried!"

"Piss off!"

"Be still my black swarthy heart and let me sing you an ode. *Oh cancer though most odious shit, keep growing where and whence is fit. In lung and liver, crevice and crack ... don't give up till she's on her back.*"

"Tomorrow I intend to do a ritual to get rid of any cancer in my body. Perhaps you would like to join me?"

"Maybe. What's in it for me?"

"That's for you to find out."

That night the woman goes to bed feeling totally spent. Whatever the outcome, she is leading a full, rich life ... whatever the hell that means.

THE BOOK CLUB

"The woman is schizophrenic ... she needs therapy!"

I am in a group of ten people sitting at an oblong table in a large room at the back of *Books On View*. In one corner, painted trees surround a stage which features a *faux* window and a *chaise longue* draped in velvet from which poetry is read aloud. The room smells like the dust cover of a haunted house.

The group is discussing my book. I cannot speak until after they have finished ... those are the rules.

"She needs counseling on finances."

"That bit goes on much too long; we get the picture without a long list of debts."

"Some parts are excellent, but it's like having a taste of cream and wanting more. I love some of the descriptions. I particularly like, *She wears her shoulders like earrings.*"

"She must be a very large woman, to want her husband on her knee; it's a bit odd too. I mean who would want a husband on their knee?"

"She could stroke her daughter's hair ... or comment on a mole or something, just to give that personal detail. My daughter has a mole on her chin ... and it's beautiful to me."

"The bit about God and evil is like God 101 ... everyone knows God is also Evil!"

"She must keep the same characters going throughout the book."

The woman thinks how impossible this will be ... for starters, Frank's restaurant has closed and the big bloused waitress disappeared. Besides, in her life people come and go.

Gradually the comments thin and their eyes rest on the woman for a response. "A lot of the book is based on fact," she starts, wishing her voice was not so hoarse.

"Come on lady, tell the truth." This from her dark side while she is in mid-sentence is very off-putting.

"Some of it is autobiographical, except my daughter does not have AIDS."

"Don't start disputing the facts now you idiotic half-wit."

The woman feels unsure of what to say next. Why is she here in the first place? To get more feedback that she is a good writer? To help finish the book? What is the point? "There is no point." Her dark side feeds on the angst. "When will you get off the pot, stop attending workshops and be published?"

Her voice squeaks, "I want to show it's important to integrate the dark with the light."

Ten pairs of eyes scrutinize her. Two people left just before her piece was critiqued. One of them apologized for leaving early, but the other had neither spoken nor allowed eye contact. When the woman had sat next to him at the beginning of class, he squeezed a long breath between closed teeth like a depressed python. His coffee cup took up two spaces but he did not move it to make room for hers.

"Yeah, yeah, yeah, he was the one who turned his back and crossed his legs away from you."

"I felt rejected!"

"No one can reject you—except you. He's probably never had an orgasm and doesn't get hugged; he would reject anybody. But you who must have all the world sing your praises before you believe in yourself, you, the immaculate turd-ball must take it personally."

"It's hard having a manuscript critiqued by strangers!"

"Don't be a writer then, dumb twat. The whole point is to have your words read by other people." The woman ignores her dark voice. Logic is okay as long as it's her logic.

At 2:30PM the leader says, "that's it for today! Here are next week's manuscripts." A stack of thin sheaves pass from hand to hand. "Please read them before next week," he adds.

Chairs scrape, bodies rise, belongings gather. Three women create intimate space by rounding their backs as if they are at a small watering hole. Scraps of words tantalize the air, '*must be paid … younger than … he never did … is she…?*'

The leader comes over to the woman. Before he can speak she asks, "Should I make changes to Chapter One before writing more?"

"No. Just carry on." He smiles with his teeth. "Lots of writers never get beyond the first chapter. They think they have to get it perfect, but you can do that later ... just get everything down first." The leader is a *corn on the barbecue* kind of guy, fresh-faced with a button down check shirt and sex in the bedroom.

"He's different from your husband who is a, *sit on my cock* kind of guy. That's why you can't look into his eyes when you have an argument," says the dark side.

"Why?"

"You're embarrassed by the primordial urge to be hunted down, gripped on the back of the neck and rammed until your bum has the purple hue of a baboon's ass."

"I hate the thought of woman melting into submission under brutal assault. I can't watch movies like that."

"You think it."

"But the thought doesn't belong to me, remember? Thoughts are like bits of software roaming the airwaves, looking for a human system to download into."

"They download into you every second of every cocking day!"

"But I know where the escape button is."

The dark side hates the analogy between humans and computers. The dark side feeds on emotions ... computers are too logical. "Let's get back to your story, butt nugget."

The leader asks, "Do you want to come to the next workshop?"

"Yes."

"Tell the truth." The dark side sounds like a Spanish Inquisitor. "The image of the man turning his back will stop you."

The woman has no strength to argue. She thanks the leader, gathers her belongings and goes for a pee. The restroom is off a dark hallway full of boxes and wrapping paper. She sits on the pot and thinks of the tribal women Silva told her about. "They can pee standing up mom, it's incredible!" The woman will try it in the shower; see if she can make one steady stream without it running down her legs.

Outside, painted in shadow, waits Doris, a woman who does not waste breath on chitter-chatter. As they brush past each other, Doris brings her face in close and says, "Your book is very powerful, you must finish it!" The woman takes the words home and polishes them every now and then, especially when she is feeling low.

The next day, the woman moves her computer downstairs. The small upstairs writing room has become intolerable with the heat. Now she sits at ground level under a rattling overhead fan and looks at closed blinds which keep the neighbors at a distance.

"Why are you afraid of neighbors?"

"I dunno."

"It's not very priestly, is it?"

"I have so many people in my life, I don't need neighbors."

"Even more un-priestly."

"I talk to them off and on, we just don't mingle a lot."

"Now you're defending yourself, I must have hit pay dirt."

The woman has read that people born on her birthdate are filled with guilt. She decides to rid herself of it once and for all. "Okay, you're right. I don't talk to the neighbors a lot. I'm friendly with them, I know their names, we exchange plants. I am a good neighbor and I will not take your guilt crap any longer. So stuff it."

The dark side snorts a laugh, "Emotion, emotion, wonderful."

She wakes very early next morning and goes to her writing room.

"Tell them why."

"Otherwise, I lay in bed and compose a whole conversation in my head, fall asleep and forget it."

"Who gets you out of bed?"

"I do."

"Don't I play a part in it?" The dark side has a big ego.

"No." She hears her husband moving about in the bedroom next door. They will live on the ground floor until the top part of the house is renovated. She tracks his movements into the bathroom, the splash of pee drilling the water gets her strangely excited. He comes in with his dressing gown open and his penis pointing straight ahead.

The woman laughs. "Let's go!"

"As fast as that?" He follows her and watches as she throws herself face up on the bed. They make love gently and softly. Small kisses that savor the closeness, they smell each other's faces, the scent of lemon and musk drifts into her nostrils. After, they talk.

"But you want praise!" The dark voice is strident. You want your ego stroked."

She ignores the voice and says to her husband, "Did you read it?"

"Yes, I finished it last night."

"What do you think?" Getting information from Steve is like popping a champagne cork ... sometimes it spills out in great bubbling sentences, other times it slides out like a slow leak.

"I like it."

The woman questions him.

The dark side interrupts, "Your husband is a saint. He takes too much crap from you."

"I take a lot of crap from him."

"Does he ever ask for a divorce?"

"No."

"But you do. Every time you argue you ask for a divorce!"

"He knows I don't mean it."

"Lady, you play a mean game. In fact, you are a mean spirited harridan."

"You know what? I've had a great morning so far. I've written some of the book. I've had great sex. A gigantic bowel movement..."

"Which you inspected!"

"...and I don't need you telling me how bad I am."

The woman feels like a wolf standing ground against an intruder. She takes a deep breath and looks at the clock. Ten forty-six. It's time to get ready for the temple and her guru. A bit of meditation will round the morning off very nicely.

"Except you forgot to run again this morning!"

BURYING THE DEAD

"Jordan's left me!" It's 1:45AM and instead of going to her apartment from work, Silva has come straight home. Her face looks like a baby rabbit with its eyes puffy and closed. "He wasn't even going to tell me ... but I knew something was wrong when the answering machine was silent ... he erased our voices." She gets tissue from the bathroom while the woman dresses the sofa with sheets, duvet and pillowcases. Silva comes back, and climbs under the sheets fully clothed.

"Don't start with the advice!" The dark side knows the woman too well.

"It's okay, I'm just going to listen."

"He read my diary." Silva covers her crumpling face with hands that remind the woman of her mother's fingers: long and able, stretching across Messianic piano chords at Christmas time. How beautiful her daughter, with wide, full mouth that at other times turns up at the corners. "He said I'm evil, that I've ruined his life."

The woman remains quiet, patting her daughter's knee.

"I'm back to square one ... living in Lake Forest with no friends." Silva sobs into recycled tissue that could be softer ... the woman continues to pat. After a while her husband walks in pretending to be a sleepwalker, with his arms straight out in front and dragging his feet like Frankenstein's monster. Without looking up, the woman moves to Silva's feet to make room.

"They wait for Silva to speak. "I knew he could read my diary at any time, I don't know why I left it there."

"Maybe you wanted him to read it," says her dad.

"Maybe. I have no friends, I can't make relationships work. I'll be living back home again." She repeats the phrase like a mantra.

Her dad says, "You have to get this *no friends thing* out of your head. It's not reality."

"But I don't have any! This is my high-school town, I should have friends here. I'm such a loser. I'M BACK TO SQUARE ONE!" This, spoken like a five-year-old on a losing streak at Monopoly, makes Silva break into a smile, but not for too long. "I have no friends."

"Born of a mother who sticks out in Lake Forest like a turd in a punch-bowl, I feel sorry for her," chuckles the dark side.

"You have friends, you just don't know it." The man walks across the room and throws his body onto the love seat so that it bounces like a small trampoline. "My butt is aching," he says. There is no reply.

The woman kneads her fingers between Silva's toes. When she feels no resistance, she continues along each foot, pressing and prodding until they are supple as pizza dough.

"I lie all the time." Silva lets her thoughts ramble. "I lied at work last week. I told them I needed the day off because I wasn't well. That I had a pain in my stomach, that my mom had an operation for cancer, that I was worried I may have it."

The woman laughs, "Am I going to die?"

"No mom, I'm just a liar."

The dark side keeps strangely quiet on this subject.

"I've learned that lying doesn't work," Steve says in a quiet voice. "If the truth is one shape ... then a lie is a different shape ... soon you have all these different shapes in your head and you don't know which one is the truth."

"He read everything, and I couldn't even be angry at him for reading it," says Silva.

"Why not?" Both parents have the same thought.

Silva rolls her eyes heavenwards. "I lied! I said I had been practically forced into having sex when I was in Australia, and there he is reading, 'it was great!' He kept saying, 'So you had sex and enjoyed it, and you were going out with me at the same time!' He's right, I'm a liar and a cheat. The strange thing is, I feel like I'm the man ... as if I am a man saying, 'I'm sorry I had an affair... I won't cheat on you again.'"

The dark side has to speak, "Steve cheated on you and because you have this 'open' relationship with your daughter and told her about it, she assumes that all men cheat. She doesn't want it to happen to her ... so she's taking on what she perceives to be the man's role."

"Oh shut up. Perhaps she just likes sex, and wasn't really in love with Jordan."

Steve says, "You and Jordan weren't really working out."

"But it wasn't supposed to end this way."

"How was it supposed to end?"

"We would stay friends."

"That doesn't happen with an intimate relationship."

"Poppycock!" Dark side wants an argument. "Lots of men and women are intimate and when it's over, they're still friends."

"I don't know the statistics, but it doesn't matter, this is about helping Silva feel okay about herself. So be quiet."

"That's the second time you've told me to be quiet, I don't like it."

"Get used to it."

Silva's eyelids slide down as if there are heavy lead weights attached. "Thanks mom and dad. I feel much better now." The parents kiss her face and leave her sleeping. They stumble to their own bed, climb in, and as their heads touch the pillow, are enveloped in dark velvet sleep. In her dream, the woman hears her guru, "The smallest, smallest good deed done unselfishly is more precious than innumerable good deeds done selfishly."

Next morning, the woman gets up early. Unlike before when her children's problems were her own, she is now able to detach from them. As her guru says, 'Be detached but never indifferent.' At the keyboard she writes, "I am starkers, in the buff, butt-raw naked. With my back rounded and my arms perched over my key-board, I look like an old man taking a Sunday drive."

"More like a vulture picking over road kill!"

The woman looks down to inspect a body that has taken 46 years to grow. Two pointed mounds rest upon a stomach sitting atop a pink tire that wobbles like a water balloon. Beneath this surfeit of flesh is her beard and two thighs, planted like ancient sand dunes, rippled and dented.

The woman walks to the mirror. She feels more beautiful than the flesh she sees. Standing five foot three and weighing ... she has to go to the bathroom to weigh herself ... exactly one hundred and fifty-three pounds. Twenty pounds heavier than when she first arrived in the States twelve years ago.

"Go on, blame it on the American diet. Like you were forced to eat extra pancakes!"

"I'm simply letting the reader picture me the weight I am."

"A bit late for that, ass head! The reader already has a picture of what you look like!"

"My son Shyam says thin people eat half a meal and wrap the rest for later; they never eat pancakes or fattening things like that."

"What's that got to do with the price of eggs?"

"Nothing. I feel disjointed."

"What's new?"

"I ran six and a quarter miles this morning before I started writing ... it's left me feeling heady."

"Again ... I say ... what's new?"

"I'm going to write about a meeting I had recently with my mom."

"I thought she was dead," says the dark side.

"She is!" says the woman matter-of-factly. "Stop interrupting and let me tell the story—I have to go back to when I'm eleven years old. My dad has called me into the dining room. "I have something to tell you," he says.

"I only half listen. I'm more interested in the fish pond outside the window and wondering if the frog-spawn has made any tadpoles yet.

"Mom's dead." Dad speaks as if it were her fault.

"My mouth feels like all the moisture's been sucked out, I can't speak. I look at my brother but he says, 'It's true, mom's dead.' I run to my bedroom, two stairs at a time ... throw myself on the bed and sob into the sheets..."

"Yeah, yeah, yeah. Until bubbles froth from your nose like soap suds."

"A bit later, dad comes in and says, 'Come on love ... we all have to be brave soldiers.' He sits with me for a while, pats me on the back and leaves. I wipe my nose and go call on my best friend Cecelia."

"I think we get the picture ... mom's dead ... you're sad ... but life goes on."

"Now come forward to the present day. I'm meditating with my friend, Kate."

"HOLD ON! Tell them about your mom's face."

"No."

"Half of it was missing, wasn't it?"

"Just one cheek."

"Eaten away with cancer."

"With radiation. I think it was more experimental in those days."

"And it smelled awful."

"The skin was dead. It was hard for me to kiss her sometimes; half her face covered in a bandage and the other half distorted."

"It repulsed you."

"Yes and no. She was my mom, I loved her no matter what, her face was something I didn't really think about. I remember being hugged, pushing my face into her cardigan and feeling all warm and cozy." The woman sits up and says, "Stop interrupting and let me tell the story."

"Keep it lively then or I'll fall asleep!"

"So here I am with Kate."

"The one you copied the tape from?"

"Yes."

"Are you meditating?"

"Yes. Kate is guiding my inner eye to scan inside my body. I see a little black box in my lower left side. Kate says in a quiet voice, 'I ask the divine healing power to show the meaning of the little black box.'"

"It's fear." I promptly answer, "Fear of my mother's death."

Kate, who knows the history says, "You were never allowed to grieve over your mother's death. You weren't even allowed to go to her funeral. I think it's time to bury her."

"That's impossible! She was buried over thirty years ago," I tell her.

"You can have your own ceremony. Get something that belonged to her. Play sad music. Light white candles." She pauses. "Do you know her favorite flowers?"

"No! I can't believe it, but I don't."

"Don't worry, any flowers will be beautiful. Just allow yourself to mourn, and afterwards, eat something to celebrate the passing of her spirit."

The next day the woman dresses in a long white gown and sits on a prayer mat in the family room. Candles flicker life into a filigreed swan—an old brooch worn by her mother every Sunday at chapel. An envelope, gray and torn at the edges holds a card decorated with a mauve and green thistle. The card in big, carefully crafted writing reads, *Dear mom, I hope you will be able to come home soon. Mrs. Hodgkiss has been alright, and I have not got told off. The second cricket match was won since the school was built. Now we are going to the Nelsons for tea. I wish you were with us, get better.* The envelope is addressed: *Mom with love, get better.* Above it, are a pretend stamp and postmark with wavy edges. The back of the envelope has been used as a memo pad: a shopping list written by the mother from hospital. And later, in adult writing a reminder by the daughter, *Mom died May 19, 1961.*

The house is empty, but still the woman glances round the room before picking up a sepia colored photograph of her mother. Wistful, the mother looks straight into the woman's eyes. It triggers a memory of play, and running into the house smelling cooked pies and clean linen and shouting, 'Mom-eeee,' at the top of her voice. The word is such a stranger, that her lips contort around it. Calling softly at first, she tests how it sounds in the air. Soon, she is screaming, 'Mom-eee, Mom-eee, Mom-eeeeee!!' The Gregorian chant throbs in the background with celestial affirmation.

In a high-pitched child-like voice, the woman asks all the questions she never could at the time. "Mommy, why did you abandon me? Why didn't you tell me you were dying? Why was it such a secret?" The air soaks up the words until there is no space left.

In the silence that follows, her mother's spirit answers, "I did what I thought was best. I was ill for so many years, I wanted to make everything seem normal for you."

"You left me and my life was horrible. Dad married twice after you died; he never loved me the way he did when you were around."

"Look how strong my death has made you. See the wonderful marriage you have. If I were around you would have run home at the first sign of trouble!"

"You don't even know your own grandchildren." The woman looks at the soulful face of her faded mother and sobs every hurt she has ever felt.

Her mother says, "They have my spirit in them. See how beautiful they are. They haven't suffered."

As the woman's questions are answered, she becomes still; a different photo catches her eye—one taken in North Wales where the family spent their summers. The woman sees herself as a baby, cradled in her mother's arms and feels wrapped in the love of that moment.

But something is not right. Deep within, she feels the presence of the black box. She looks inwards and sees it has turned into a coffin with her mother climbing inside. "Don't get in there!" screams the woman.

"You have to let me go." Her mother peacefully lowers herself in and closes the lid. The heaviness in the woman's heart pulls her over until she sits like a hunched old crone. Outside, a robin sings its territory and a helicopter thwack, thwack, thwacks its way through air that smells of bristling nature all charged up for summer.

She has to bury her mother. In her mind's eye the woman kneels beside the coffin and hammers the lid down; then she gently lowers the coffin until it goes out of her body and into the earth far below. She throws a handful of soil over it and watches grass and flowers grow over it. Then she hears a whisper. Still with her eyes closed, she sees her mother's spirit hovering free and clear of the coffin, "See, I never left you!" it says. "I love you, I will always be with you to watch and protect you." As the woman watches, her mother's spirit gently floats away.

The woman has visited her mother's grave only a few times, but she can picture it anytime—a rectangular plot surrounded by a simple stone. It lies under the bower of a huge tree in a peaceful old English churchyard.

"In reality..." The woman knows what the dark side is going to say and prepares herself. "They have built a huge monstrosity of freeways and road junctions around the churchyard. Your mother's grave is within constant sound of trucks, road works and 24 hour traffic. I doubt if her spirit is very happy!"

"Her body has long gone from the grave ... and her spirit is free to go where it wants. Allow me please to finish my story."

"Go ahead wuss bag."

"I feel released. I open my eyes and see the envelope. I turn it over in my hands and notice mom's shopping list. For the first time I realize it's a list of flowers. French Marigold, Lobelia Cardinalis, Cornflowers and many others. When Kate asked me about my mother's favorite flowers I felt sad that I could not answer. Now I know what they are ... I can even plant them in my garden."

"So why haven't you?"

"I never got round to it."

"That's your life ... scattered with good intentions ... but totally unfulfilled. I don't know why I waste my time with you."

"I don't know either."

"Because one day you'll get it and..." The dark side went silent.

"And?"

"And nothing. Simply nothing."

MR. BOGEY MAN

"Because you have nothing to teach me!" Kate is speaking to the woman from the passenger seat of the parked car. The moon is sitting in the night sky as if painted specially for Hansel and Gretel. Kate and the woman have just come back from Ram's house, where every last Thursday in the month they have meditation.

Ram and his wife Mira are both doctors from Sri Lanka. They have a large peaceful room upstairs, decorated with pictures of dark-eyed, long-bearded Indian gentlemen. A gold and red mandala hangs above an altar on which stand small blue jars with candles that flicker onto the dancing figures of Shiva and Gonesh... Eastern gods.

Standing at the back of the room, Ram beats the heels and fingertips of his hands against the skin of a tall slender drum. Sitting cross-legged, his delicate wife picks the strings of a beautifully carved and ancient sitar. Between them, the rhythm sways back and forth sewing itself into the air. The nine other people in the room begin to chant, "Om Namo Bhagavate Vasudevaya!" Starting slowly, the chant builds layer by layer until it fills the room with a solid pattern of sound. Like an orgasmic vibration, it becomes so loud and fast it feels as if the threads must break.

The woman's head turns from side to side in rhythm and she becomes completely free of all thought. The music plays for another fifteen minutes. The drum is the first to slow, its powerful cadence calms the room until all fall into a meditative silence which extends for almost an hour.

A few months earlier Steve had come to chant with them, but after the first ten minutes, wrenching cramps drove him to the bathroom where he spent the next hour in the violent throws of diarrhea; he never came back to another session.

"Don't get off the subject." The dark side jumps in. "Tell them about you and Kate."

"Okay, okay! Don't rush me..."

"You silly cow! You have to make this book a page turner or it will never sell!"

"Yeah, yeah, yeah! After the meditation, everyone went to the kitchen for herbal tea and popcorn ... everyone except Ram and Kate that is."

"Were they having sex or something?"

"Of course not."

"Why of course not? Remember that young woman who lived in a local Ashram and the so-called Guru kept having sex with her; it's a sexual energy thing—Tantric yoga or something."

"Well, they were just talking."

"Don't tell me the thought of hanky-panky hadn't crossed your mind ... all that chanting, energy, openness, fecundity!"

"I admit, I did have the fleeting thought, in fact, I wondered what Mira, his wife was thinking, but she didn't seem to be aware that Ram was not in the kitchen."

"And my name is Snow White!"

About twenty minutes later Kate and Ram walk into the kitchen. "What have you been up to?" I try to make my voice light and joking.

"None of your beeswax!" replies Kate with a smile. She's almost always smiling. Her eyes, big green orbs, shine out of an attractively imperfect face and her large wide mouth sits under a small upturned nose that manages to look regal and aquiline. I feel squat and shapeless by comparison.

"Have another doughnut!" The dark side sniggers.

The woman ignores the voice. "In the car on the way home, Kate tells me, 'Ram and I are exchanging work. He's giving me a cranial sacral healing, and I am doing his astrology chart.'"

The woman feels green bile rising from her belly into her throat.

"That's because you are a very jealous person." The dark side enjoys these moments. "Other people would be overjoyed that their friend was happy. Especially if they need healing."

"I know that! That's why I feel so lousy."

"So tell me precisely what happened."

"We get to her house and I put the car into Park. She's talking but all I can think about is my jealousy and that I have to speak out."

"If you don't it will grow into some awful disease ... like CANCER!" Her dark side will not give up on the old tape but the woman ignores it.

"I turn to Kate and in the half darkness she reminds me of my best friend, Jean, from way back in high school; I'm always drawn to lively, beautiful women."

"So you can feel outshone by them. It's called setting yourself up as a victim."

"I have something I need to say," I tell her.

"What is it?" she asks.

"I've known Ram for a couple of years now. He came to my ordination. You see him twice and you're already exchanging healings. I don't understand it."

Kate replies, "I have a charisma that attracts people to me. It's what I do. I work with people." The woman remains silent as Kate continues. "Your strength is in your writing. It's a lonelier existence, but it's very powerful. I can't even construct a letter, I have to ask you to write my flyers for me."

The woman knows this is true, but still ... she doesn't feel satisfied by the reply.

The dark side interrupts, "You're letting her play a number on you."

"I don't think so. It's true what she's saying, I'm a writer, not a talker."

"You're not even much of a writer to be honest," the dark side chortles.

"Although..." The woman thinks of all the talks she gives. "I talk to my meditation group. I give healings and help people neutralize old karma!"

"But you don't have the same charisma as Kate." The dark side cuts at her mind like a pair of French dueling swords.

"You're right... I don't!"

The woman waits for Kate to break the silence. "Remember when I channeled that image of you as a little old Egyptian man with the long white hair?"

"Yes."

"He was so old, he couldn't get all his wisdom out; so he reincarnated in you."

The woman knows she should feel good about a little old Egyptian coming back to write his wisdom down with her help, but she doesn't.

"That's because it takes away from you." The dark side interrupts her thoughts. "If some little old Egyptian is doing all the work, then what are you doing?"

"Please keep quiet, it's confusing to have you keep butting in with your comments."

"I have noticed you want to control me more, but you will never shut me down completely." The dark side makes this final comment before taking a back seat.

"Being a writer is a lonely existence, but you need to accept it." Kate tells the woman what she already knows. "I need to be in front of people ... it's what I do best."

"But that's what I want too. I want to give workshops and have interaction with people."

"You're good with people too. People like to be around you."

"See, she's contradicting herself now." The dark side refuses to be left out. "You know yourself better than anyone, but you continue to let people talk as if they know everything about you." The woman tries to ignore the voice. "Remember when Kate told you that she wanted to be a REAL priest, as if your priesthood wasn't real, remember how you felt then?"

"I felt really bad inside."

"You like being manipulated."

"I don't."

"Yes you do, otherwise you wouldn't allow it."

"I guess I don't FEEL like a REAL priest," says the woman. "Even my dad reminded me that it takes at least four years in England to be ordained!"

"And you feed off that, but what you don't understand is that we're all playing roles, and sometimes our roles don't seem real to us. Do you think I like being the dark side all the time?"

"Yes."

"No. Sometimes I want to be light. But I have to accept my role as dark."

"You could integrate the two."

"That's blasphemy."

"It's what I want ... harmony and balance," says the woman.

"Not as long as I have a voice, ducky."

The woman wants to get the bad feelings about Kate out of her, and the only way she knows how is to tell Kate everything she feels. She turns in her seat so that her knees point toward Kate. "I feel jealous of you and I hate it. I don't want to feel this way. It's the same with my eating, I want everything. I crave things and I want to stuff my face. It's pure greed!"

The woman has spoken to a friend of hers, Sandy, who is losing weight through God. Sandy attends a Bible study group, where they point to all the places in the Bible where greed and gluttony are highlighted, and how there is no bad food, just greed and gluttony! The woman thinks she might go along and see if it can help.

Suddenly the car door opens. "Mom, what are you doing? It's spooky you sitting in the car in the dark." Kate's seven-year-old son, Kenny, has blond fresh hair that curls away from his smooth, pink face; he looks like a cherub.

"It's okay darling, we're just talking. I'll be in shortly." Kate leans toward her son and kisses his nose.

"Mom, can Patrick and me walk to the end of the driveway?"

Kate pauses for a moment. "If you're both careful."

Kenny and his little friend move into the shadows and are soon lost in darkness. Kate laughs. "Look at them both, it's their great adventure, walking to the end of the driveway." Kate lives in an enormous house on a three acre lot. The driveway extends back to the house and the three garages. Kate turns to the woman now. "I think it's a childhood thing. With your mom dying, and your dad not really bothering with you or showing you much affection, I think you crave attention."

This feels right to the woman so she lets Kate continue. "You have a hole, so you fill it with food and anything you think other people have."

"How do I get rid of it, this hole?"

"You have to give to yourself. Look at me, I go to workshops, I have healings because I know I'm worth it! I mean what's this silly nonsense of you not buying clothes for a year!"

"It was an agreement I made with myself."

"But why? Why wouldn't you want to make yourself beautiful?"

"I don't know. I don't even have manicures anymore." The woman pauses to remember why she is depriving herself, "It's because I want, need, to save money."

"But what's $20 here and there? If you don't give to yourself, nobody else will." Kate pauses and then adds, "It stops you from giving to others as well."

It makes sense to the woman. Yet, the times when she gave too much of the wrong things to herself are still very evident: Her wardrobe is jammed full of clothes she will never wear. Old silk dresses that would turn even Cher into a frump. Tight skirts she can't wriggle her bottom into. Long hippie dresses that make her look like a bag lady. Why does she hang on to it all?

"Because it stops you from being the powerful woman you want to be." The dark side loves this kind of talk.

"The whole 'power' thing is really old. Power doesn't come from clothes."

"You think you introduce yourself with words? Cock Fodder! Everything about you shouts out who you are to the world. The way you sit, the way you walk, the way you behave, the way you stand, your handwriting, your way of speaking, your way of wearing clothes, your way of looking, your way of letting your body be in this world, all this shows what kind of a person you are. You don't have to introduce yourself!"

"It's hard though."

"For a dingbat like you it would be."

"I would like to wear clothes I feel comfortable in. Throw away those I don't like."

"It'll never happen to a nimrod like you."

"I need to recognize that I am already powerful. I'm like Judy, I don't understand my own power."

Judy called round earlier in the week. She's directing a small skit in a local amateur production. "I'm having a real hard time with the people," she admits.

The scene is almost the same as a year ago when they were sitting in the kitchen having a cup of tea. That time, Judy sniffed a couple of times, screwed up her nose and said, "I smell gas." For the next few minutes, they both inhaled so deeply their nostrils squeaked like high pitched flutes.

They discussed whether it was more stupid to call the emergency gas number and find there were no leaks, or not call and die from asphyxiation. Finally, they called and a gas man was there in five minutes. He found seven leaks in the ancient stove ... and cut the whole supply off. The woman was without a stove for three months because they had no money!

"Get on with the story, wuss bag. Why is Judy having a hard time?"

"Half the people don't turn up for rehearsals." The woman goes on to describe Judy. "She has long brown hair tied back with a ribbon, she has a great figure and controls her eating without problem. She can sit a six inch chocolate cake on the counter, cut herself a small slice, eat it, put the rest of the cake in the refrigerator and leave it there untouched until the next day. If anyone went round with a bag of cookies and offered her one, she would say, 'No, I've just eaten, you have it!'"

"She hasn't learned the *how to stay fat* concept," sniggers the dark side.

"What's that?" The woman rises to the bait.

"To keep going no matter what. To eat and eat until your stomach feels so stuffed you want to throw up... It's called being a pig!"

Judy says to the woman now, "One man actually said to me, 'You need an adult diaper!' He used a laughing voice, but I could tell he meant it."

"I don't understand. You're really funny. You could get them to do anything you wanted."

"I suppose so." Judy didn't sound convinced.

"She's like you. She doesn't use her talent." The dark side goes back to an ancient theme. "She thinks she has to be very serious to be powerful ... she doesn't see that her greatest power is in making people laugh. Remember that story she told you..."

"About the tin bath."

"Yeah, that one."

Judy had been to a parents meeting at her son's school. "And there I am in Lake Forest at 8:00AM," she says, "sitting with all these women who look band box fresh, talking about their housekeepers. I hate going into their houses; I never know where the bathroom is. With them it's, 'You need the bathroom? Oh yes, keep going along that corridor until you reach the west wing, take a right and it's the fifth door on your left!' I nearly wet my pants by the time I find it!"

"Well, you are in one of the richest suburbs and you do send your son to the Lake Forest Academy!'"

"I know, it's ridiculous. When I think about my aunt with her tin bath hanging on a nail in the kitchen. I had a bath there every Friday night; that's when the insurance man would call. He'd knock at the kitchen door and my aunt never had the money ready." Judy lifts her purse up and hunts in it as if she is her aunt looking for the insurance premium. "There I was sitting in the bath covering my private parts with a wash cloth and the insurance man standing at the door pretending not to look. It was a different world."

"Oh God, I know," says the woman laughing. "One time my dad had us pee in a bucket in the kitchen. When it was full he threw it on the lawn to make the grass greener." The woman recalls it with mild wonder. It sounds like something made up.

"My aunt did the same thing! She had a bucket full of pee and tea leaves under the kitchen sink."

"What did she do with it?"

"I don't know... I suppose it was thrown out with the dishwater."

"But why did you all pee in the bucket if she just threw it away?"

"Because she shared an outhouse with Mr. Bogey Man; there's always a Mr. Bogey Man when you're growing up."

"Oh God that's right, we had an old couple who lived across from us, and if our ball went into their garden it was lost forever; nobody dared go and ask for it back!"

"We never went into my aunt's out-house in case we got trapped with Mr. Bogey Man at the other side shouting to get in."

"You're so funny. You could earn a living telling stories."

Judy swirls her tea leaves round the cup as if they are going to tell her something awful. "Yes, I suppose so."

The two women talk about England and how different it is from America. "I had an American friend who visited England and kept seeing a sign which read, 'REFUSE TIP'. She couldn't understand why people would refuse a tip—until one day she realized *refuse* meant *garbage*—it was a sign for a garbage dump!"

"I know!" said the woman laughing at the strange differences between English and American language.

Later that morning, Judy phoned, "I'm going to be really powerful at the next meeting. I'm going to take no nonsense and I'll expect them to do everything I say."

"Why don't you just use your humor? It's your most powerful tool. If you come across all 'no-nonsense' it'll get up their noses again."

"Yes you might be right. I'll use humor instead."

Just then, the woman's husband comes into the writing room and she is catapulted back to the present time. "How are you doing?" he asks.

"Fine." The woman feels the story has come to a stop anyway. "Would you like to read it while I go take a shower?" He sits down at the computer and she shows him how to move the print up and down the screen.

"What did you think?" she says, later standing showered and naked except for a towel wrapped around her wet hair.

"It's great. Very readable."

"Do I sound mean spirited?"

"No. You sound normal."

"I never hear Kate talk about anyone in a bad way. Everyone in her world is wonderful to her. Healer friends come and stay with her just to be around her energy; she really is a joy to be with!"

"Sure, and my name is Rumplestiltskin. She gets angry, and vicious. You should start seeing the world as it really is."

"I keep thinking of Maria in the Sound of Music, so fresh-faced and vital; I want to be like that, to have a voice like Julie Andrews!"

"I suppose you think Maria Von Trapp actually sewed all seven play suits for the children out of curtain material in one night! Imagine all the buttons and zips, the nightmare!"

"You're right of course, but how wonderful to feel like sunlight all the time." The woman stares out of the window for a while then returns to her own characters. "What about Ram," she asks her husband. "Does he sound like a big walking cock or something?"

"No," says Steve. "But I don't get the bit about Kate, when she says at the very beginning of the conversation, that you have nothing to teach her!"

"She was telling me about walks along the beach with her psychic friend and the incredible conversations they have. And I said, Why don't you walk along the beach with me? And she said, 'Because you have nothing to teach me.' It made me sad, that's all."

"But you do have things to teach her. Did you ask her why she thinks that way?"

"No."

"Well then!" Instead of throwing his hands up, her husband walks to another room.

The woman sits back at her computer. She does feel sad that Kate will only walk along the beach with her if she has something to teach.

"It's your ego again." The dark side wants the last word as usual.

"I suppose one day I'll realize my oneness with everything; I will experience the unity and harmony of the universe and love will be my most immediate and natural sensation."

"What a dork!"

The woman can think no longer. Shyam got home last night from working in New York and they are meeting Silva downtown for lunch. She will talk these matters over with them, unless of course, they have bigger problems to solve!

SOME ALCOHOLICS NEVER DRINK

"I'm an alcoholic." The two couples are in a swanky Chicago restaurant eating dinner. "I don't tell everyone." The woman is sitting across from Todd who is making the confession between mouthfuls of pasta covered with walnut and cheese sauce.

"I didn't know," says the woman.

"You are a liar." The dark side doesn't let her get away with a thing.

"I heard some rumors, but I never saw him drunk or anything."

"When you saw him round town, you knew something was wrong" says the dark side.

"Yes, but just keep quiet while Todd speaks."

"He nearly died." His wife, a tall woman named Katrina is squeezed in the narrow booth beside her husband. "His ulcer popped, it was touch and go for days."

"It took me ten months to dry out," says Todd.

The woman's lower jaw drops open. "I never knew."

"It's the quiet lives of secret lunacy." The dark side snorts a laugh. "You all spend so much time trying to put on a brave face; whole lives are consumed by intrigue."

Steve turns to Todd and says, "Why did it take ten months?"

"I'd been drinking for so long, I was about 22 years old when I first started. I remember the very first time. I was meeting my buddies and I went into a bar to get a quick drink before we met. After that, every time I went somewhere, I had to have a drink first."

"He was shaking so much in the hospital, my son and I spent five days holding him down."

"I thought I was flying." Todd puts his arms out like a small boy pretending to be a airplane.

"Flying?" Steve and the woman both speak at once.

"I was driving cars, planes, boats; I felt like I was flying the whole time."

"One time I said to him, 'look Todd, I'll drive for you.'" Katrina takes hold of his arm as she speaks.

"And I said, 'I can't let go of the steering wheel!'" They both laugh at the memory.

"How are you now?" The woman is glad Steve has asked the question.

"I go to AA meetings in Lake Forest. You would be surprised who goes. We have a secret kind of wink when we meet." Todd laughs and squints his eyes.

"I didn't know there was an AA in Lake Forest."

"I've been to them in Florida, the Bahamas, they're everywhere."

"It's strange," says Steve, "but you being an alcoholic makes you more sober than the rest of us. You don't touch a drop now, yet you have to keep saying you're an alcoholic."

"Once an alcoholic, always an alcoholic."

"So how did you dry out eventually, what made you realize?"

"The woman who owned the place where I went to dry out was about 86 years old. It's her whole life, making people better. She would say to me, 'Todd, don't be a child!' She knew I was a load of bullshit. That I wasn't doing it."

"She was great. Much better than a psychiatrist." Katrina pulls her face as if the word tastes of sour pickles dipped in sand.

"Psychiatrists are hopeless," agrees Todd.

"Why?" says the woman, amazed.

"They don't even know the symptoms of alcoholism. They just want to give drugs."

"What's wrong with drugs?"

"Well see," Todd puts his fork down to illustrate the importance of what he is about to say, "if I rely on alcohol to get through my life, what's the difference between that and drugs? There is none!" He picks up a glass of water and takes a small sip. "If I take a drug that makes me feel better, a little thing goes off in the back of my head which says, 'drugs made you feel better, why not have a small cocktail, then you'll feel even better than better.' It triggers something in my brain to keep on drinking."

"So what's the answer?"

"AA. It's the only answer." Todd looks at them intently. "I go to a meeting every night."

"Wow. Every night!" The woman has no concept of how it must be to struggle every day with drink.

"I have to. People have no idea what it's like to be an alcoholic. I used to hide the small bottles, the miniatures you buy at Walgreens; I hid them in my office where I thought no one would look. Then I'd forget where I hid them, and spend the entire day looking to find them before my secretary did."

The dark side sidles into her mind like greasy pasta. "So what are you really thinking about these people?" It wants to know every detail.

"It's frightening. Talking to someone who has gone off the deep end; it's hard to communicate without feeling I'm in a TV drama."

"Ask Todd about his dark side."

The woman says to Todd, "I'm writing a book about my dark side, but in a way I feel kind of lame after listening to what you've been through."

"I used to look into my face," Todd leans his head forward with his eyes wide and staring as if he is peering into a mirror. "I saw so much darkness I thought I would never get out."

"My dark side is something like..." The woman searches for an example, "standing in this restaurant, and shouting, 'Fuck off all of you and get a life!'"

Later in the car on the ride home, Katrina says, "Have you ever heard of Tourette's syndrome?"

"Yes." The woman realizes Katrina has been speculating about her shouting 'fuck' in the restaurant.

"I told you not to let people know what you're thinking, dickwad." Her dark side has a thing about not letting people know the intimate details inside her head.

"The truth will set me free—besides, I had to disclose a secret about myself, since they had told so much of their lives."

"You'll never learn."

Katrina continues, "I told Todd, if I ever start shouting things out like that, kill me!"

They ride in silence passing trees, and houses with rooms holding countless lives. The woman thinks of what Todd said earlier about his wife, "We're balanced now." He had said, "She's done stuff too. Lot's of stuff!"

Katrina had looked down at the table cloth. "I used to drink heavily. We had horrible arguments. We would finish work, go to Walgreens, buy a bottle of voddie and promise each other we wouldn't argue."

"You drank in the car on the way home?" The woman cannot imagine being so hooked on alcohol.

"Why not?" interjects the dark side. "You do the same with chocolate you gluttonous, greedy pig!"

"Yes," continues Todd, "by the time we got to the overpass, we were already arguing."

"It was a bit further than that," says Katrina. "Usually by the time we got to Highland Park."

"No, it was way before then!" retorts Todd.

The woman thought how strange to argue about the minor detail of when exactly the argument started.

"It's funny," Todd picks at the food around the edge of his plate. The sauce has congealed and lost its shine. "But we always argued about exactly the same things. Exactly the same things."

"They never changed!" agreed Katrina.

EROTICISM

They are curled like spoons in bed when her dad brings his arms
around and strokes her nipples. In her dream she is 12 years old
and flat-chested, but even so, her breasts pop up like hot kernels
of corn as she thrusts them forward for oiling. She wants him to
fill her hole but instead, he moves away and goes to the bathroom.

"Your cunt has been licked by the devil's flame!" Her dark
side penetrates her dream.

"I'm wicked."

"Not wicked enough for me, baby."

"I feel like a scum bag having dirty dreams like this! I'm
trying not to have them."

"Try? Nobody ever achieved anything by trying. Try and pick
up a pen! You either pick it up, or you don't. There's no in between, no trying!"

The dark side is right. The stirred up feelings do not go away.
When she does make love to her husband, she feels she is
making out with her father. She feels so ugly, she can't even tell
Steve about it.

"That's because you think it will shock him."

"Maybe."

"But you told Kate."

"I didn't intend to, it just popped out."

"Aha! Weakness leads to talkativeness!" says the dark side.
"You need to learn to zip your mouth up; but there is no danger
of that happening." The dark side sniggers and sits back compla-
cently.

"We were meditating as usual in our little group," continues
the woman. "And one of the women Emma, says, 'I had this real
strange dream last night. I dreamed that my clit-o-ris...' Emma
pronounces the word as if it belongs in a medical journal, 'grew
into a penis. My husband Edward was there but I knew it would

gross him out, so I kept trying to hide it from him.' I told her it was her male energy and that she was frightened of him seeing it."

"It kept growing and growing!" said Emma extending her arms as if she is holding a huge, giant cucumber.

Into the silence the woman said, "I had a strange dream too." She describes her sexual dream about her father and finishes by saying, "When my mom died, I was alone in the house with my father and brother and I think I was frightened of the male energy, like I had to take over mom's role, with sex too."

No one asked if they had sex, but she felt a need to respond. "Nothing ever happened. My brother and I, when we were little, well he liked to clean my belly button out because it was so deep and got filled with fluff, but nothing ever happened, I just liked the attention."

"You didn't get titillated?" The dark side wants every detail.

"I knew it was a bit naughty, but my brother would never do anything to hurt me, he never went further than my belly button."

"And your father?" The dark side wants to explore everything.

"Nothing. I vaguely remember wanting to sleep with him after mom died but he said I couldn't."

Emma said, "It must have been very difficult for you, I had a similar thing; my mom was an alcoholic so it was like she was missing. There, but never present."

The woman continues with her own train of thought, "I always locked the bathroom door, afraid my father or brother might see my body, or me see theirs. I was mad at my dad and it was awful because he would sing in the mornings, and I would tell him to shut up!"

"Why?" The dark side keeps interrupting with the questions other people will not ask.

"For not being a mom. The house was a pig-sty."

"Why didn't you clean it?"

"I never thought about it, except one time when I invited three school friends home for lunch. I spent hours scouring the kitchen; cleaning the dishes. We brought fish and chips home but still, I was embarrassed about my home."

"Your dad cooked for you?"

"Yep, he was a professor at the local college, he cycled home with meat or fish; he used to make steamed suet pudding in a handkerchief, and we covered it with golden syrup."

"And you never helped?"

"I don't remember. I hope I did."

"Why don't you ask him?"

"He doesn't talk about his life before Francoise, his third wife."

"What happened to wife number two?"

"They got divorced. I hated her for a long time. She seemed so mean. But last year, my brother and I went to visit her in Kent and this little 81-year-old lady opened the door."

"What did she say?"

She asked us in for a cup of tea and showed us her paintings. "Come and see my studio?" She was really proud of herself, and we followed her upstairs to a back bedroom where all her paintings were stacked against the walls and floor. She gave us each a small watercolor. Before we left, I put my arms around her and said, "I'm so sorry for everything that happened between us." We both cried.

"I really loved your dad," she said.

After that, she wrote my brother saying, "I'm sorry about your dad. I can't believe he doesn't care about his grandchildren. What kind of a father can he be?" The letter went on as if we were all going to gang up against my dad, so my brother wrote back and told her dad was really okay, and that we still had a reasonable relationship.

"How was she mean?" asked the dark side.

"It seems silly now, but she had a daughter five years older than me who didn't want to come live with us. She didn't want to share a room with me, so my step-mother hung a pink velvet curtain down the middle of the bedroom. My step-sister got the window and the pink velvet side of the curtain. I got the wall and the lining."

"And you've kept it like a nasty little memory tucked away all these years?"

"Yes."

"That's where a cancer will start."

"So help me get rid of it."

"Can't, shan't, won't!"

"I'll stop conversing with you." The woman remains silent and goes into the kitchen to prepare lunch.

When she comes back the dark side says, "I'll help you a little bit."

"Okay."

"You have to say the forgiveness ritual."

"What's that?"

The dark side describes it. "Sit facing east and bring the person you need to forgive into your sun center, the space between your eyes, just above the root of your nose. Say the words, *I forgive you for anything which you have knowingly or unknowingly done to hurt me. Please forgive me for anything which I have knowingly or unknowingly done to hurt you.* Turn counter-clockwise, face north and repeat the words in each direction. It's very powerful." The dark side is quiet for a moment. "I'm only telling you this as a favor, I don't want you to think I'm turning soft or anything!"

"Of course not!" says the woman.

Next morning, her husband walks in the room while she is writing about the dream with her dad. She moves the mouse so he can't read the screen.

"Go have your run," she says. "I can't write when you're looking over my shoulder." He pulls his bottom lip into a pout and she says, "Read it then!"

"No, you finish it." He blows her a kiss on his way out. A few minutes later he's back.

"What is it?" She laughs at his tall, thin figure dressed in tight black running gear, like some desperado plucking up courage to rob the town bank.

"It's so cold out there." He holds one sleeve to his mouth and one to his ear as if talking into a telephone, "Hello, hello, is there anybody out there?"

She walks over and hugs him, "I love you. Just go do it." He laughs and jogs out of the room. She waits until the front door has closed before resuming her position at the keyboard.

A minute later she hears footsteps. Her son Shyam calls, "Mom? Mom are you here?"

"Yes I'm in here, dad's gone for a run."

"I'm going for one too." Shyam's short black hair sticks up like twigs caught in a gutter, but even though he has just woken up, his fresh, clean face shines out of an untroubled soul. He looks at the screen and draws closer. The woman surreptitiously repositions the mouse so that an entire conversation moves up the screen.

"I notice..." The dark side sneaks up, "that you cover up the fact that you don't want him to read your work, while for your husband your maneuvers are quite obvious."

"Shyam's more sensitive."

"Balls! You're the insensitive bastard."

The woman ignores the voice and says to her son, "Remember the Cabala that I told you about?" Shyam's face looks as blank as the top sheet of an 8 1/2 x 11 stack of cream, 20lb. xerographic paper. "When I told you about the Tree of Life?" Still blank. "When I was teaching you the Tarot cards!"

"Isn't it the hardest thing, having to explain things? People should know what's going on in your head." The dark side points out a truism so she doesn't feel the need to respond.

Meanwhile Shyam pretends that a light bulb has gone on. "Oh right," he says.

"Remember the 22 Paths that connect the Tree of Life?"

"Yes."

"You know he doesn't remember, don't you?"

Again the woman ignores the voice.

The woman turns to Shyam, "I've just done a word count and I've written 24,865 words in 11 chapters. So by the time I've written 50,000 words which is a decent book length, I'll have done 22 chapters: it's very mystical."

The dark side interrupts, "It's true that books intended to illuminate the mysteries of God, are sometimes arranged in twenty-two parts. For example, *The Book of Revelations* has twenty-two chapters, and St. Augustine's *City of God* has twenty-two books. But really my dear, I hardly think we can compare them with your little piece. It's not even in the same stratosphere!"

"No one is asking you. I'm simply pointing out the mysticism."

Shyam dresses in his father's old running gear kept in a large wicker basket. Balancing on one leg he pulls the stretch black fabric up his muscular legs and sings in a Sunday chorister voice, "So you'll make lots of money then?"

"I don't want to write it for money though. I don't want to seem desperate."

"Oh go on mom, be desperate, do it for the money." Shyam's open face makes it seem perfectly okay.

"Do you think so?"

"Yes. Why not?"

"So when it's done I want lots of money."

"Good, mom."

When Shyam has left the room, the woman adds to herself, "I also want health and happiness alongside the money."

"You are so wimpy," the dark side sniggers. "It's your stupid Protestant work ethic. You're frightened that if you get money, you will lose something."

"Right."

"Look stupid, you'll never get money, have no fear."

The woman returns to her writing. Something about retelling the dream of her father has triggered a memory.

"Maybe you blocked some horrible memory of your father and brother screwing the arse off you every night." The dark side slobbers over the words and the woman feels her mouth fill with saliva. "Maybe you were used like a *fille de joie!*"

She swallows and replies, "Nothing like that happened."

"How do you know?"

"I just do." But the woman knows there is a trace of something not right. "I remember lying in bed with dad and feeling ... I don't know ... hot and dark." The woman tries to remember but she can't tell if it's dream or reality.

"It would make sense why he's ignored you all these years. Guilt is a big thing."

"But nothing happened."

"It didn't have to. Steaming erotic thoughts under the bed-clothes is enough to bring down the wrath of God."

"I remember him telling me not to come into his bed anymore."

"There you go!" The dark side smacks its lips with the relish of being right. "And remember what your first stepmother said when she saw you in the kitchen hugging."

"I had just come back from France. Of course I hugged him. We never hugged normally, but it was a special occasion. I was very glad to see him."

"And your stepmom said, "If you love her that much, why don't you take her to bed with you?"

"I felt really bad. Like I was a sick puppy or something."

"And you are."

Shyam calls through the house, "I had to come back, my ankle is hurting again. It's stopping me from keeping fit." His voice gets louder as he reaches the writing room. "It's a bummer."

"I know. My left thigh has something wrong with it. I haven't run for over a week."

"He isn't interested in your left thigh, you dickwad. He wants sympathy." The dark side seems to like Shyam.

Shyam comes in and kisses the woman on her left eye and begins to peel off his running gear. He takes his jockey shorts off and puts them over the dogs head so that the crotch is against the cold black nose. "Awww, don't do that," says the woman, but the dog sniffs happily and looks almost disgruntled when Shyam whips them away.

"It reminds you of when you let the dog lick your fanny doesn't it?"

The woman had told an entire workshop of over 60 people including her husband, son and daughter about the incident. As directed by the facilitator she said, "What I don't want you to know about me is … that I let my dog lick in between my legs." It had been a relief to say it out loud, but she did not need reminding of it now.

"Why not, you dirty bitch? And I use that politically incorrect word with all due respect to the doggy world."

"Bog off. I am, what I am. I am good and I am bad, and I intend to balance the two into blissful harmony."

"You probably believe in Santa Claus too!"

Later that day she prints out the dream about her dad for Steve to read. She is very embarrassed.

"You are ticked off because he knows more about you than you do about him." Her dark side knows everything about her.

"I have a lot of stuff, he doesn't."

"Get him to tell you about his dark side."

"There's no point. His dark side doesn't trouble him."

The woman looks into her husband's face and says, "So what do you think?" There are no signs of disgust or repulsion.

"It's great."

"What about the dad thing?"

"What about it?"

"Does it disgust you?"

"No."

"And the dog thing?"

"There's millions of people whose pet dogs have licked their bum."

"But the dad thing. Do you think there was more to it, and I've blocked the memory? That happens, you know."

"If you think about it long enough, you'll imagine something *did* happen, next thing you'll be on Oprah, and your poor dad will be castigated as a child molester. Thinking is a very dangerous game!" laughs the man.

"You're right. The brain can't tell the difference between reality and visualization. That's why visualization techniques are so powerful!"

That night, the husband and wife make love. "Are you thinking about your dad?" asks Steve with a laugh.

"No, but I could do if you want."

"I don't think it's very funny to joke about it." Her dark side hates it when they joke about serious matters.

"Get a life." The woman switches the voice off and thinks about her dad. No, no eroticism there anymore, it must have dissipated. Steve slaps her gently across her buttocks. "Do that again!" He slaps her a bit harder. "Hey not too hard, this is just a game!"

"Get your ass over here and stop talking." The couple are not into hurting each other so they romp on the bed, kissing and pretending to bite.

For once the dark side is silent. Telling about her dream and talking to Steve about her dad are enough to vanquish the dark voice. A friend had asked her, "What happens after you have had the conversation with your dark side? Does the thought go away?"

"It seems to." Later that night, she reflects on her day, and thinks about the question. Does she still have the horrendous baby thought? No, she doesn't. If it does come back, it's simply as a thought, one that does not belong to her.

Again, the dark side is silent on the subject; she decides this is a good sign.

CUTTING UP CREDIT CARDS

"We have no money!"

"What's new?" The dark side is, if nothing else, a truthful entity.

"Yesterday the phone rang and a computerized voice said, *'Please hold, we have a very important message for you.'* Usually I hang up, but this time I wait."

"Next time, hang up on the bastards," says the dark side.

"Then a live person who sounds like he's just out of high school comes on and checks that I am me. 'You owe $504.00 this month on your Visa card. When can you pay it?'"

"I don't have it to pay." I keep my voice light and breezy.

"How much can you pay?" the child voice says.

"About two hundred."

"Well the past due is $364.00. Can you at least pay that?"

"I'm not sure."

"You're playing games," says the dark side. "Excellent, excellent. Show them what you're made of."

"It's so horrible, people on the phone asking for money," says the woman.

The dark side spits at her like water on hot oil. "It's their money. You borrowed it—now they want it back!"

The woman tells them she will pay the past due and ends the conversation. "Then I looked at the invoice," she says to the dark side. "The interest rate is almost 20%, and the finance charges each month are $82.70!"

"They have to make a profit somehow."

"I called them back—it was a woman this time. I told her I would never be able to pay off the credit card because the interest rate is too high. I asked if she could lower it."

"What did the cow say?"

"To call the Consumer Credit Council. She gave me an 800 number; I called and talked to Maureen."

"We can reduce your interest rate payments to 8% if you use our Debt Management Program," said Maureen.

"I made an appointment for next Tuesday at 10:30AM."

"I suppose there's a charge."

"The appointment's free, but there's a $5.00 monthly fee depending on what they do; she said we could discuss it when we meet."

"Sounds too good to be true; what's the catch?"

"We'll see."

Later that afternoon, her friend Judy sticks her head round the office door. Envelopes, bills and torn paper are scattered like dried business bones across the carpet. The woman is reconciling her Quicken accounting program. "Hi," says Judy. "I saw your car so I thought I'd pop in; I won't stay long!"

The phrase reminds the woman of her Grandma Shaw's long-ago, Sunday afternoon visits. "I'll keep my hat on thank you very much indeed." She would say, "I'm not stopping." And her hat remained stapled to her head by a large and ferocious-looking hat pin with a small red rose on one end and a two inch steel point on the other. In retrospect, Grandma Shaw, was probably afraid of contracting *hat hair:* the deadly disease which leaves a replica hat brim in the coiffure.

The woman turns to Judy and says, "Come in ... have a cup of tea." "No, really, I'm fine. I have to pick my son up in twenty minutes; I'm supposed to be using this time to buy a birthday present." They look at each other as if to say, 'So why are you here then?' They laugh and Judy says, "I'll have that cuppa!"

Their English background makes them comfortable with one another. They can talk about Merry Old England in disreputable terms without offense. "I'm paying bills." The woman points to the stack of unpaid invoices.

"Oh God!" Judy raises her huge brown eyes and rolls them upwards. "Don't get me started."

"I'm going to a Debt Management Program next week. It's only $5.00 a month and everything will be paid off in three to five years."

Judy leans forward in her chair. "For only $5.00 a month?"

"No," the woman laughs. "The *fee* is $5.00; I don't know how much it will cost to get out of debt. I find that out next Tuesday.

It's the credit cards, even though we don't use them anymore; we still owe money."

"I have one for identification, but I never use it." Judy thinks for a moment. "Actually I did use it the other day; I had the car towed; it needed a new battery but they wouldn't take cash. I was terrified in case the card didn't work." Judy holds out a shaky hand as if she is handing the card over for inspection. "I'll never forget the time they cut it up."

The woman has heard this story before, but it is so funny she is willing to stay quiet. "I was out shopping with a friend. She'd been so kind to me and she saw this pair of earrings, they were only twelve dollars. I said I'd buy them for her. My friend kept saying, 'Oh no, you don't have to.' But I insisted, so we went to the checkout and I handed my card over. My friend and I stood talking, I noticed it was taking a long time, but I wasn't worried. I didn't know how things could be, you see." They exchange a knowing look.

"You hadn't experienced credit card crap."

"Right! Next thing, the saleslady hands me the telephone and says in a snotty voice, 'They want to speak to you personally!'"

"'Hello,' I say, 'can I help you?' The woman on the other end says my card is past due and I can't use it anymore!"

"How embarrassing."

"That's not all! I say to the salesperson, 'I'll give you cash, can I have my card back please?' 'No!' she says, 'I have instructions to cut it up!'"

"Oh my!"

Judy pretends to be the saleslady speaking into the store intercom. "Scissors to checkout number four please, scissors to checkout number four!"

"She didn't!!"

"She might as well have! Everyone in the line was straining to get a good look at me—the criminal. Then she reached under the cash register, took out a huge pair of scissors and cut up my card. I got so angry, I had the money you see! I don't know why I used the card! I started to take cash out of my purse."

Judy relives the moment by grabbing her purse, pulling out a bunch of dollar bills and slamming them down on the desk. "I turned to the line of people and said, 'Look I have money!'" Judy pulls more bills out and slams them on the desk. "I have enough money to buy five pairs of earrings if I want, but I'm not going to!"

Judy bursts into laughter. "I said to the saleslady, 'I'll never buy anything from this store again. You can keep your earrings!'" Judy is laughing so much she can hardly speak.

"What was your friend doing?"

"Standing with her eyes like organ stops, probably thinking, 'But I want those earrings!'"

"Did you ever get them for her?"

"No!"

"Do you still see her?"

"No!" A fresh burst of laughter. "My parents don't understand credit cards. They pay cash for everything."

"Yeah, my dad's the same." The woman suspects it's a generational thing.

"Jim came home the other day and said we should take a few days off to see the fall colors in Wisconsin, but we don't have the money, we owe bills. How can we spend money on fall colors, when we can't pay the electric bill?"

"I know."

Judy continues, "My mom and dad would never do that. My brother and his family moved into a new house that had a naked light bulb hanging in one of the bedrooms. My mom couldn't believe they went on vacation and left it hanging there 'til they got back. When my mom and dad go away, everything is left spic-and-span, bills paid, house in order..." Her voice trails off as she thinks about the gulf between their world and ours. "I got a delinquent notice from the mortgage company yesterday. A delinquent notice! In red!" The women derive great comfort swapping money stories.

"What did you do?" The woman recoils.

"I'd already paid it." Judy moves to the edge of her chair and straightens her back. "These mortgage companies are so big they don't know what the heck they're doing. There's probably a little woman up in room 5207 handing out delinquency notices, and all the while, down in room 2545, some young fella is holding onto my check and hasn't bothered to tell room 5207 that he's received it!"

The woman pictures a huge tower full of people toiling away their lives on paper work.

"I called them up." Judy puts her hand to her ear as if speaking into the telephone. I said, "I've already paid, why don't you communicate with each other? You should work in a smaller place."

"What did she say?"

"Oh I didn't really say those things." Judy laughs, "I would like to have said them, but I didn't."

Steve walks into the office changing the atmosphere from summer to fall. It's impossible to talk about money with their menfolk around. Hunters of his age feel inadequate when reminded about money problems; after all, they are supposed to bring home the bacon, the loot, the readies, the spondulux!

"Hi Judy, hower-ya-doin?"

"Great."

He turns to his wife and says, "Will you be long?"

"Are you going to let him talk to you like that?" The dark side was enjoying the money talk. It's the one thing that consistently causes animosity and struggle. "He's a manipulative male chauvinist, isn't he? Coming in and breaking up your talk."

The woman swallows and replies to her husband, "I've got to finish these bills, print out some chapters, then I'll be home."

"Okay. I'll get the bread and shopping then."

"Great!"

The woman turns to Judy and asks, "Do you know the time?"

Too late, she remembers Judy once saying, "I hate people who don't wear watches; they want to be free of time, but expect other people to wear them! When they ask me, 'Do you know the time?' I look at my watch and say, 'Yes.' Then I just stand there. They get quite upset and say, 'Well, can you TELL ME what time it is?' As if I have nothing better to do! Now, when someone asks me, I give them the wrong time!"

"It's okay, I've got it on my computer ... it's 4:45 PM."

"Ooh is that the time? I've got to go," says Judy.

"And I have to get to the post office before five." Steve rises from his chair and says to the woman, "I'll see you back home then ... in...?"

"About twenty minutes," she answers.

Later that evening, they have dinner at the kitchen table and the woman tells them about her upcoming appointment with the

Debt Management people. "How much do I owe on my credit card?" asks Shyam.
"About $1200," answers the woman.
"I need to pay it off."
"That would be nice."
"Where is the bill?"
The woman reaches for the bill folder and hands Shyam the invoice.
"19.80% interest!"
"Yep, that's how they get you."
"If I cancel it, then I don't have to pay the interest rate, right?"
"No dear, it doesn't work like that." The woman realizes she has fallen down badly on educating her children about money. "You have to pay the interest until the whole amount is paid off."
"So why do we have credit cards?"
"Because they give you a credit rating. You can't get a mortgage if you don't have good credit." The woman recalls the problems when they first came to America; they couldn't open a bank account because they had no credit history. She turns to Steve and says, "You know that Sears account we opened to buy a new washing machine?"
"Yeah."
"It's 21% interest, so with the minimum payment of $22.00 and a finance charge of $17.00, we're only paying off $5.00 a month! It'll take us the rest of our lives to clear the debt!"
The family turn silent.
"It will never end!" The dark side revels in the sorrow and despair. "You will always have money problems because you draw them to you like flies round a turd."
"Flies eat crap, they are an important part of the system. I can learn from my money problems."
"How?"
"I don't exactly know yet."
The woman wishes she could make up some wonderful fairy tale analogy, but she can't. Life is a balance, and not everyone can be a star, except in their own mind!

SCREW WORMS & NIGHT SOIL

The gray-haired figure is desolate and bent over crying. Nine swords stacked horizontally overhead symbolize failure, disappointment and possible death. It is one of the worst cards in the Tarot pack.

Outside, leaves fall and a fragile beam of sunlight dances across the pine knotted kitchen table. Sunny, whose name belies her somber personality says, "It's the death and transition of your dark side."

"Hey, I'm not going anywhere!" The dark side is very defensive about its death.

"I don't think it means you," says the woman. "It's my death ... probably cancer."

"What question did you ask?" Colleen is a welcome addition to the Tarot class; she has a face that makes a person shine inside.

"I asked whether my book would be published," says the woman.

"Obviously not!" chimes in her dark side.

"I thought you'd want it published."

"I've hidden all my life; I'm not ready for exposure." The dark side slinks away to ponder the future.

Although it's morning, a candle glows soft against a pink quartz rock and exotic spiraling sea shell—long lost home of a now-dead crab. Burning incense completes the carefully designed ambiance. "To me..." Laney, a woman of indeterminate age and carefully measured words, says, "the swords are not actually piercing the flesh, so whatever it means you have free will to change."

"You're right." The nervous rasp in the woman's voice is noticeable only to her own ears. "We can always change our future with balanced self-conscious awareness."

"Pompous little ass-hole!" But the dark voice is easy to ignore when she is teaching.

She instructs her class to reshuffle their cards and lay the 22 Major Arcana on the table. The Devil is the first card she turns over.

"That's because Tarot is the Devil's game." She ignores the voice.

"Tarot is interpreted as The Royal Road," she says, "and the Trump cards tell the story of our soul's path through eternity. It begins with The Fool, innocently setting off, not even looking at the path."

"My Fool is about to fall over a cliff!"

"Mine is holding a flower."

"What about the dog?"

The woman takes a slow, deep breath and begins, "In the ancient world we thought fools were closer to God than other people. The simpleton doesn't have to deal with the complexities of everyday life so they have a better set of values and a clearer perception of God. Even the word *silly* means *blessed*."

"St. Paul said, '*let him become a fool that he may become wise.*'" The group looks at Colleen. "I studied with a Bible group for many years." A delicate blush like a 'tea-rose' lights up her face.

"That's exactly right." The woman leans forward with her elbows. "But most of us want to be right all the time; we think it's ignorant or naive to be innocent so we pretend to be sophisticated and know everything. Did you know sophisticated means artificial?"

In the short silence Colleen thinks about the Fool's dog. "Dog spelled backwards is God!"

"It could symbolize a longing for God." For the next hour the woman teaches them until they reach card number 15, *The Devil* again. A noxious amalgam of human and animal parts that make her feel she's hallucinating on Bridge Mix and TV dross. She describes the card: "The Devil, like God of ancient times, is depicted as male, and stands on a platform to which two smaller demons are tied. He has the horns and legs of a goat, the wings of a bat and holds a burning torch in his talons. It is a symbol of the power of evil in the world. Humankind held captive by our own animal urges, materialism and the dominance of brute force and ignorance. The Devil upholds pride, hatred, cruelty and lust."

The dark side raises its head. "It has great creative power and intelligence."

"Yes, but it uses them to selfish and wicked ends."

"Like charging money for meditation, house blessings and Tarot lessons?"

"That's how I earn my living."

"No dearie. You earned your living writing video scripts and training programs for $15,000 a pop! $10 a lesson is not earning a living!"

"It's what I want to do, and if it's God's purpose, I'll be taken care of."

"You see God as some Great Grandfather figure with a white beard sitting on a fluffy cloud!"

"I see God as a force of energy that lives inside and outside of me. We are all united in God. The trouble is, most people think God is something very different and more powerful than them, but if we could see ourselves as part of God, we would see God in everything and everyone around us. We would stop cutting ourselves off from other people and judging them as some lower form of animal."

"So who am I?"

"Part of God."

"Like Lucifer, the bringer of light!"

"Whatever."

Three days later on a bright Sunday morning, the woman and her husband drive south to the Temple for the *noon meditation*. The car feels safe and isolated as she shuffles the Tarot cards back and forth, filling them with her personal vibrations. Finally, Steve asks, "Are you going to pick a card?"

"Okay."

"What's your question?"

"Do I have cancer." She shuffles and cuts the cards thinking, 'If it is a good card the answer is *no,* and if it is a horrible card, the answer is *yes.*' She holds her breath and turns the top card over. It shows a person lying face down on the ground with ten swords sticking out of its back. The sky is filled with black clouds and a dead tree hangs over the body. It is the worst card in the pack, even more ominous than Nine. It means death, ruin, disaster and the failure of all hopes and plans.

Steve asks, "What did you get?"

"Disaster and possible death!"

"It probably means the death of your dark side." Steve tries to be positive but the lines between his eyebrows deepen.

She reads the interpretation aloud, "Extreme wariness is essential and no one should be trusted."

"Will you pull a card for me?" It's a couple of years since Steve asked her to do a reading because he always used to get the Tower card: struck by lightening, two figures fall to their death, symbolizing the destruction of a false system of values.

The dark side moves across her mind and whispers, *"I saw Satan fall like lightning from heaven."*

"Excuse me?" replies the woman confused.

"Jesus' words, not mine," answers the dark side.

"I didn't know you quoted Jesus."

"To obtain perfection," says the dark side, "all existing things must be annihilated. Lucifer is merely the author of destruction, his lightening flash destroys error. As P.D. Ouspensky—the leading disciple of G.I. Gurdjieff, the famous Russian mystic and teacher—stated, *'If only men could see that almost all that they know consists of the ruins of destroyed towers, perhaps they would cease to build them.'* Your husband is at the stage of the advanced seeker for wisdom who suffers the destruction of his former philosophy."

"Does that mean his life is built on shaky foundations?" asks the woman afraid of the answer.

"That's for me to know and him to find out," smirks the dark side, feeding off the doubt.

The woman asks Steve to choose a card. With his eyes still on the road, he reaches out and blindly picks one. It's an angel pouring liquid from one cup to another while bright golden light shines over outspread wings. *"Temperance,"* says the woman. "A wonderful card. It symbolizes the bridge between spirit and flesh. It means you have a guardian spirit helping you understand your own special quality and power."

The dark side says in a very solemn voice, *"'Strait is the gate, and narrow is the way, which leadeth unto life, and few there be that find it'* That's what Jesus said."

She looks out of the car window, "How will all these people, in all these cars ever find their way?"

"They'll find it—just like we will," says Steve.

"I know," she replies, wondering if they will.

The temple is an old house on Kedzie. Three years ago, in its third-story tower, she was interviewed for the seminary.

"Tell them about Tim." The dark side loves gossip.

"There's nothing to say."

"You were going to ask him to be your teacher but there was a sex thing going on in your head."

"But that's all it was."

"What did you say to him?" asks the dark side eager to review old anxieties.

"I said, 'Tim, I'm afraid if I become your student, I'll become sexually attracted to you.' It's happened before, you see."

"To which he replied? ..."

"I never go to bed with my swamis!"

"He didn't get it, did he?"

"No."

"It triggered something in his head."

"It felt sordid the way he said it."

"He never talks to you now?"

"It's sad—he's a really nice guy but he's put up this big wall."

"You need to bring your feelings out into the open."

"I'm afraid to, he probably thinks I'm a slut."

"He's probably right!"

"Let me get back to my description of the temple. On the second floor is a chapel, painted sky blue with clouds on the walls and ceiling. I sat there cross-legged every Sunday morning for two years, it was like being in heaven. The main temple is downstairs. A big blue silk cloth with a white circle in the middle, hangs down from the ceiling above the ... well I guess you could call it the pulpit, but it's a raised platform with two large candles, flowers and a chair.

"A swami dressed in white with an orange and red shawl draped across his shoulders gives the noon meditation today. It's about finding joy in every moment. 'Don't be worried about the future or get caught up thinking of the past, be happy now!' he says, 'my girlfriend talks very slowly, and I am often tempted to finish her sentences. Sometimes I do, but what I say is never as good as her words, so I've learned to be patient.'"

"Sure!" says the dark side. "Anyone with half a brain can see he's not patient."

"At least he's aware of his shortcomings. Be quiet!"

"When I overtake cars," says the swami, "we all end up at the same stop light anyway, so what's the point of rushing? I may as well be easy on myself and my car."

"I bet he goes over the speed limit." The dark side has a heyday at the temple. "It's great to see pious people up close."

"Shhh! I'm missing bits."

"My mom and I were visiting my brother in Georgia and she lost her upper teeth," continues the swami, "so my brother cut the meat up real small for her, but she was still having trouble eating. He said to her, 'Ma, come into the kitchen and we'll put your food in a blender and you can tell me when it looks right for you.' I thought about him later, it was such a caring thing to do. To be patient and loving."

After they leave the temple they meet Silva and Shyam for lunch. The woman talks about Tarot cards and Steve says, "Tell them about the question you asked!"

The woman feels hummus and pita bread regurgitate into a small burp. It escapes unnoticed to the rest of them, but leaves a sour taste in her mouth.

"Go on, tell them."

The woman swallows, "I asked if I would get cancer."

"And what was the answer?"

"Yes!"

Silva says, "It's heredity, isn't it?"

"Some is."

"And you had ovarian cancer?"

The woman is shocked, "No! Where did you get that idea?"

"That's why you had the hysterectomy."

"No. It was pre-cancerous."

"Oh!" Both kids look relieved.

"I really don't think I have it. And if I do, *C'est la vie!* I'm not afraid to die."

"You aren't going to die," Steve says. "It was over eight years ago; if something was going to happen, it would have happened by now."

"True."

"But you're not convinced are you?" Her dark side sidles into her head. "There's still that tiniest bit of you that thinks a little cell might be brewing trouble in your body."

"Get stuffed. I've just come from a great meditation about living in the moment and feeling joy, I refuse to be brought down by you."

By the next day, all the words are forgotten when Steve and the woman begin an argument about her never being on time. Shyam who is present finally says, "I hated it when I was small and you argued. It made me really frightened. And now, it feels exactly the same."

"I'm sorry Shyam." Their apology is spoken together, as if on some higher plane their 'timing' is perfect.

"If only he didn't think he was always right!" The woman can't let go.

"You said you would be back at half-past-four," says Steve. "We waited until five-thirty and you still hadn't arrived." Steve is determined that she see his point.

"You're right," she concedes. "I was late and I'm sorry." If the woman could zip her mouth it would be okay, but she can't. "I didn't know you were waiting for me. I could have had dinner at Kate's; I thought you were out running."

"Is she always late, dad?" Shyam the Libra tries to find some balance.

"Yes!"

"Are you, mom?"

"Yes."

"Dad, you *are* anal about time." Shyam hopes his dad will take some responsibility for the argument.

"We have a duty to be on time," he responds. "I think she does it on purpose to upset me."

"I do not."

"She doesn't, dad."

"Being late is a form of aggression. It's a way of having power over other people who are then forced to wait!" Steve goes on. "When I teach people, I expect them to be on time; if they come in late for a class they're in trouble!"

The woman wishes she could return to the calm of the temple. It was so peaceful floating in her inner being. Why is it so difficult to come back to reality, to time, to husband, to Steve!

"You haven't been getting along too well recently." Her dark side gloats at the opportunity to delve into a problem. "You don't really love him, do you?"

"Yes I do."

"What about Saturday when you were cooking and baking up a storm and he was watching TV?"

"I hated him."

"But why? Does he have to act as your baking assistant? Pass the paprika, chop the chives."

"No. But the front porch needs painting, he could do that."

"You decided to strip the paint, then you realized it was too big a job; you left it half finished for 18 months!"

"I want Steve to fix up the house, to do some of the painting."

"It's not in his nature."

"Now he reads all the time, like his mom. This morning, he was still in bed reading at 8:45AM."

"So what?"

"To be a successful public speaker, he needs to edit his video tapes so he can send them off to agents, but he wants someone else to make him famous."

"He needs your support?" The dark side has got to the nub of the matter.

"I have supported him! I made a lot of money writing scripts and training programs. I can't do it any longer. I want to write my own stuff. Be my own person."

"If it wasn't for him you would be in deep doo-doo." The dark side enjoys the conflict.

"He is too lazy to be successful."

"That's not true. He makes lots of telephone calls, sales calls, he trains people how to negotiate, how to sell, he's very busy. All you do is sit at the keyboard?"

"I cook, I keep the house clean, I do washing."

"He washes and cleans house."

"He vacuums and wipes a surface, but his hand has never actually been down the toilet bowl!"

A few days later after Steve has painted the porch the dark side says, "You really are a heap of cow dung. Look at Steve, he's painting! Working! Cleaning! What are you doing?"

"Writing a book."

"Idiots write books. I tell you what?"

"What?"

"Pick a card and see what it says about your writing."

The woman picks, 'The World' and says, "Ultimate spiritual reality. Great Work accomplished by God and by human kind ... or in this case ... me!"

"I have a quote from Ouspensky, *'It is the world, which we always see, but never understand.'* And you my dear, do not even see it!"

"Help me then."

"You must learn to accept the *night soil,"* retorts the dark side.

The woman looks up the meaning in *Webster's New Collegiate Dictionary.* *'Night soil—From being collected at night— excrement removed from a cesspool or privy and used as fertilizer.'* "But how much *night soil* do I have to dig through before I find light?" she asks.

"It never ends. Day follows night, follows day, follows night, and every so often there's a full moon."

"I don't understand."

"Read some Carl Jung: *'If attention is directed to the unconscious, the unconscious will yield up its contents like a fountain of living water. For consciousness is just as arid as the unconscious if the two halves of our psychic life are separated.'"*

"It has to be much clearer for me to understand." The woman is confused. "Maybe I need therapy?"

"You don't have the money."

"True." The woman sighs. "I just hope you're not screwing me up too much."

"You are right to use caution, I am a kind of Screw-worm... I get inside things."

The woman reaches over to Webster's again, and reads, *'Screw-worm—Cochliomyia hominivorax—an American blow fly that infests wounds and the nostrils, navel, etc., of animals, often causing illness.'* Ugh!

"Don't worry, I'm not the cause of your illness."

She didn't know why, but she was beginning to trust her dark side a tad more. Perhaps it was because it made her examine herself more closely. Whatever the answer, she was much more comfortable talking with it than she had been.

"Don't expect me to have nice cozy *gabfests* with you!" The dark side does not want to become a confidant.

"Course not," says the woman, "once the book is finished, you can go away for good."

"Don't be stupid. I'll always be around."

"Oh." The woman wonders how such an antagonistic relationship could last into the future. "Perhaps we can be friends then?"

"No dearie, never friends, something much deeper, something too simple for your complex mind to grasp, but then again, you're so naive you might eventually get there!"

THE INTERNAL PIPE

"I can't stop eating!"

"What do you weigh now?"

"156 lbs!"

"You've put on another three pounds!"

The woman has brought this problem to her dark side because she has nowhere else to go. If her dark side is the negative force in her life, and over-eating is negative, then maybe she can put that force to good use.

"I don't see how I can help you." The dark side is not interested in helping.

"Show me what I'm trying to hide from."

"Hide from?"

"I'm going to tell you a story," says the woman.

"You have five minutes, and no rambling."

"I was at a place called Angel Fire near Santa Fe, building a sweat lodge, or as Wallace Black Elk, the Lakota Chief who was with us, called it, a Stone People's Lodge."

"Get to the meat! Damned dufus." The dark side does not want spurious details.

"I was snug and warm in my hotel room, it was 3:00AM. Next thing, I wake up and hear someone call my name. There's nobody in my room so I look outside and see a huge full moon shining down on me. *'Come here!'* It says."

"Don't tell me. You go outside even though the hotel is in the middle of a thick forest, it's black as Pharaoh's tomb, and big bears hang out at the garbage cans!"

"I couldn't ignore it."

"You're a lunatic!"

"Well the moon is lunar," laughs the woman. The dark side is silent so she continues. "I dress, walk to the field in front of the hotel, sit on the grass, pull my hat down, hug my knees to my body for warmth and look up into the face of the moon."

"Get on with it."

"Softly, she says to me, *'Speak the truth, speak the truth, speak the truth!'* She repeats it over and over until I must have heard it a hundred times."

"This is the moon talking?" sniggers the dark side.

"Yes."

"Go on."

"I say back to her, I'm afraid, I'm afraid."

"We get the picture."

"The moon tells me not to be afraid, *'Hold out your hand and touch me,'* it says."

"You're a real space-cadet aren't you."

"I close my eyes, make my hand into a fist and extend it toward the moon. My hand opens and I feel as if I am touching the surface of the moon. It feels cool and protective, like I have nothing to fear."

"Even though it's black as tar and there's bear in them their hills?"

"Right."

"What happens next?"

"She tells me to walk into the forest."

"Lucifer help me."

"I am really scared, I see a bear in front of me. But the moon repeats, *'Don't be afraid.'* I walk toward the shape and it disappears. My fear lifts with each step and I am filled with spirit. I see spirit in the trees, the air, the dark, the light, the animals, the earth, the sun and the moon."

"What kind of spirit, you huge geek?"

"The creator, the God, Goddess. It is part of me and I am part of it. It is within my power to draw whatever I need from life toward me. I will find the teachers to show me the way, and I will choose what I need to learn. I realize the importance of speaking the truth."

"He who speaks the truth, walks alone," says the dark side in a macabre voice.

The woman ignores the voice. "I can draw positive energy from within me. Then there are the angels."

"Angels are old news, faggot face."

"Old or not, they are around me and I need never be afraid again. It is one of the most exhilarating experiences of my life."

"Doesn't take much, does it?"

"As I walk back to the hotel I am given more truths. I know why I am 20 lbs. heavier than I should be. My soul is so fearful it has built up my physical body as a protective shield."

"That's why you eat negative, clogging foods."

"Yes. Dark foods that have a lot of sugar and fat in them, like chocolate."

"But even when you come back from Angel Fire, you don't lose weight, do you?"

"I want to eat food that has grown in mother earth, that has been nurtured and fed by the sun."

"But you still get fat."

"I become a vegetarian, and lift my vibrations higher. It's like being in the crow's nest of a schooner. I see everything so much clearer."

"It all sounds well and good but you are still overweight!"

"I'm trying to lose weight, though. I'm on a cleansing program eating vegetables, fruits, brown rice, whole wheat, pasta, nuts and legumes."

"It won't last."

"You want me to argue, but I won't. I'm studying foods. Choosing vegetables to suit my moods."

"Which are many and varied."

"Chocolate makes me feel loved, then mildly depressed and wanting more chocolate. But crisp, succulent veggies help me relax, lighten up and feel clean. My guru said that we can never satiate our greed; if I crave chocolate, I just want more and more, I will never be satisfied."

"Is this a cook book you're writing?"

"No."

"Then get off the stove—it's boring."

"Okay. I'll talk about the other end."

"What other end?"

"There's a pipe runs down the middle of our body and has two ends; it starts at the mouth and finishes at the anus."

"There's lots between your mouth and your ass-hole."

"Yes, and that's why people who walk round with mouths sucked up like dried prunes, have bowel problems. We have to let go of our mouths and smile."

"Then what?"

"Then our ass will smile. They're connected don't you see? I had bowel problems because I was in my head too much. Now I smile more, don't take life so seriously. I have good bowel movements."

"Life is not that simple, you big titty."

"It is. We just make it more complicated."

"Is this going anywhere?"

"Yes."

"THEN GO!!"

"It's about my colon cleansing."

"Okay, this is interesting."

"I'd heard about it, of course, but it always sounded disgusting."

"Having a tube rammed up your ass and filling your bowels with water sounds like exquisite torture to me."

"I go to a place in Milwaukee. I drive into the parking lot and three women wearing green aprons ask me if I would like to be escorted to the clinic. I reply in the affirmative."

"This is not a legal document, so please keep it simple. Still, it's rather odd to be escorted to a place where they execute bowel movements!"

"Exactly what I thought. But, we're not talking the same clinic. They take me to an abortion clinic!"

"And you with no womb! How delightful."

"I tell them there is some mistake, that I am here for a colonic. They realize I need to be next door. They point to a small place, rather like a health food store. I ask why they are escorting people. The woman tells me that anti-abortionists picket the clinic. I look across the street and see a man holding a placard painted to look like blood and dead fetus."

"How does it make you feel?"

"Macabre. I wonder why men are so involved with unborn fetuses when they could to be so involved with the issues of living children, but I let it go and walk into the colonic center where I am met by a woman named Crystal."

"Welcome, may I take your coat?" she says softly. We sit under a picture by Monet of a woman with a blue parasol taking a child for a walk through a field of poppies. "Let me tell you about *Intestinal Management*. There is no doubt," Crystal says, "about the relationship between the intestinal tract and the rest of the body; some of the most important functions of life take place in the intestines. As a society we should all be more bowel-wise! Come with me and I'll show you where we will be working."

"We walk into a room filled with incense and harp music."

"It must be hard to make a bowel cleansing place anything other than what it is?" The dark side enjoys a story about feces.

"This is the bed you will lie on." Crystal points to a narrow bed of the kind usually found in a doctor's room, a beauty salon or massage parlor. She explains what will happen. "You will undress from the waist down, lie on the bed and cover yourself with the paper blanket."

"Same as a gyne exam but without the stirrups!" The dark side snickers.

Crystal leaves the room so that the woman can undress; she re-enters the room about five minutes later. "Okay. Are you comfortable?"

"Yes."

"Then lie on your side and relax, while I insert the tube."

"The tube goes up my rectum quite easily, it feels strange but no pain."

"Pity." The dark side links physical and mental pain together.

"I'm going to turn the water on now." Crystal talks in a soothing voice. "Say when you want me to stop."

"I feel really scared. Thoughts zoom round my head like, *What if the water won't stop and I get filled up too much? Where does the water go? What if it comes too far up my body and I start coughing up water mixed with shit?*"

"How are you?" Asks Crystal.

"Fine!" I lie. "Suddenly I get the overwhelming feeling to let go. Stop! I shout."

"It's okay," says Crystal. "Just let go."

"I feel a deep gurgling evacuation in my bowel as if I have been holding on to an underground water fall. It's even deeper than the usual satisfaction I experience in the bathroom."

"You mean you don't have the actual feeling of poop sliding out your ass?" The dark side wants all the gory details.

"That's just it. There's no sensation of taking a dump. Just a feeling of letting go."

"Do you fart?"

"Yes and no. I hear water and gas sloshing through the tube as I evacuate my bowel, but it's not gross."

"What about smell?"

"Nothing."

"Then what happened?"

"I talk about you."

"Me?"

"Yes, how I was blocked in my guts and that I'd had cancer and I was worried it was still there."

"What did Crystal say?"

"That I would clear it all away by doing a couple more colonics."

"And have you?"

"No."

"What a Loser!"

"I've been too scared to go back. But I have felt a lot better since I went. I don't have the pain in my left side anymore. In fact I'm going to make another three appointments right now."

"I'll believe it when I see it."

The woman leaves the writing room, picks up the phone and dials Milwaukee. If there is one thing she has learned, it is to use her intuition. She will cleanse herself of this stuff inside her mind and body. And this time, she will use the help of others.

One week later the dark side asks, "So did you make the appointment to have another three colonics?"

"No. There was nobody there."

"You are just too perfect for words."

"Why?"

"Falsehood personified. For example, when you say to a friend, 'I'll meet you next Saturday at 9:00AM.' What you really mean is, 'I probably won't meet you. I will most likely cancel at the last minute.' Your word is not your law."

The woman thought about this for a moment. "But I don't want to make another appointment to have a colonic!"

"Why say it then, dumb head."

"Because it seemed like the right thing to say at the time."

"That's because you say things without thinking. Look," the dark side coils around her inner ear. "It's okay to be the way you are. You are a free spirit. You don't need to be organized, that's for people who don't have a life. You are free to do what you

want, when you want, and with whom you want. Change your
mind as often as you like, it's good for you."

The woman wonders if she should make the appointment after
all. It's the money, she tells herself. She doesn't have the money
to pay for another three colonics.

"Exactly! You are not worth spending any money on. Body
work is for the bees."

"I am going to make those appointments, and from now on
my word is my law. What I say, I will do. This is my agreement
with myself and I expect you to help me."

"Me?" The dark side sits up with a sharp jolt. "Me help you?
You must be out of your mind."

"If you don't I will lock you away again and never bring you
out."

"Okay. But I don't understand how I can help. It's not in my
nature to assist."

"You can remind me to think before I agree to do something.
You would be good at that."

"Something like, 'Hey numb nut are you sure you want to
commit to this?'"

"Yes, I can live with that. But you have to remember to do it.
Can I count on you?"

"I'll try it for a while and see how it goes."

"Okay."

"So numb nut, do you really want to have another three
colonics?"

"I'll have another one, then see how I feel."

"Good enough."

The woman looks at the clock, it is 7:24AM on Wednesday
morning. The place does not open until 10:00AM. Will she
remember to call for the appointment? It is time to take charge of
her life and her mind. Time to stop making excuses. Time to get
off the pot! "Life is not a rehearsal, we only get to play it once,"
she says in a schoolmarm's voice.

"What about reincarnation?" The dark side sniggers. "I
thought you wanted to come back as something spectacular next
life time."

"I'd rather be spectacular this life time, be counted on to do
what I say I'm going to do."

"Your stab at logic tires me. You are still too emotional to amount to anything."

"I'm working on it."

"How?"

"Meditation."

"That's why some mornings you meditate and some you don't. You enjoy living on a roller coaster; you think it's passionate to be up and down, happy and sad."

"This is one psycho-bubble I'm going to pop." The woman clicks on *save*, and turns off the computer. She wonders if she should accept the way she is, foibles and all, or change herself into super-swami: healer *extraordinaire*. The word God pops into her head and she looks across at the ancient Bible lying on the table. She opens it and reads the official scroll on the inside front cover, *Methodist Sunday School, Presented to:* Her father's name is written in faded ink and underneath the date she reads, *July 15th, 1934.* She opens the book at random and reads, '*And David said unto him, How went the matter? I pray thee, tell me. And he answered, That the people are fled from the battle, and many of the people also are fallen and dead; and Saul and Jonathan his son are dead also.*'

"What does that mean to you?" The dark side doesn't hold much with the Bible.

"Battles kill, that if I keep having this internal battle with myself, I will soon be dead."

"So stop."

"That's why I acknowledge you, and when I have put you to rest I can get on with my life."

"What if I don't want to be put to rest?"

"Then you have to be listened to. I assume you have a voice because you have something worthy to say." This is the first time the woman has talked about her dark side having something worthy to say. It feels strange. If the dark side is part of her, then she is killing part of herself.

"You will cease to be fully whole."

"ENOUGH ALREADY!!" The woman closes the Bible and walks out of the room; some things cannot be answered all at once, and that, she decides, is perfectly okay.

IN GOD'S HANDS

"The problem is that Steve is a liar and a thief."

"I really don't want to get into this"

"You can't keep it hidden—I won't let you." The dark side has been rummaging around in this deepest garbage for a while now, and the woman has been trying to suppress it.

"I'm afraid to write it down. Steve pulled the Nine of Swords followed by the Ten the other day." I looked it up and it means prison."

"So?"

"I woke this morning thinking about what it would be like to go to Jail."

"And how was it?"

"Okay. I could teach meditation, do healings and preach sermons."

"Save us from the missionary sickness."

"I am more afraid for Steve."

"Why?"

"In men's prisons they commit buggery; I'm afraid other men will…"

"…want to take a hike up his bum?"

"No."

"Do you think he's gay?"

"He might have had bisexual thoughts; I know that when he was a boy scout they all took turns masturbating the scout leader."

"How pleasant for the leader."

"But that was a long time ago; I don't think they do that kind of thing around the executive table."

"So what about his lying?"

"His father lied, so Steve thought it was okay. He's done it since we were married, been unfaithful, caught out, I've talked about this before, it's old hat now."

"And when you came to America he swore he was completely faithful?"

"Yes."

"But you don't believe him?"

"We had a couple of Welsh friends called David and Megan. She was a very attractive outgoing female, and he was a quiet, dour sort of man."

"So what happened?" The dark side is intent upon getting the facts and nothing but the facts.

"Steve liked to go out with them, but I wasn't keen. When it was their wedding anniversary, Steve arranged to take them to the Mayfield Hotel, he was working for corporate America at the time. He did a lot of work with the hotel, sometimes he arranged private functions and put it on the company bill."

"Thievery and corruption is rampant in corporate life!"

"It's a perk!"

"It's thieving!" The dark side knows where to draw the lines.

"Anyhow, we took them there for their wedding anniversary and I was telling them we belonged to the Mile High Club!"

"Fucked in the clouds!"

"It was in the bathroom of a 747 jumbo jet."

"And Megan said...?"

"I'm surprised you fit into the bathroom at your size."

"She's quite a mean person then?"

"It's all said with humor, I should have laughed and taken it as a joke."

"What did Steve do?"

"Nothing."

"Were you mad at him?"

"Yes."

"What was he supposed to do, punch her in the mouth?"

"No. I wanted to stop seeing them, but a few months later Megan turns forty, and her husband asks Steve to put on a big party for her at the Hotel. He's talking about having a male stripper, the whole works."

"Why would David ask another man to arrange his wife's birthday party?" asks the dark side.

"If it's free who wouldn't? But I refused to let Steve organize it. Instead, we arranged for a few friends to meet at Megan and David's house as a surprise party."

"Steve wasn't happy though, was he?"

"It wasn't a great success. Kind of lame really."

"So what made you think Steve and Megan were an item?"

"David got moved to Arizona; the whole family went and Steve talked about how we could perhaps move there one day!"

"I was so blown away, he never mentioned it again."

"Did you visit them?"

"No, but they visited Chicago one time. They booked into a hotel downtown; it was Friday and Steve and I were going into the office together because I was writing his company's annual report. That morning I got dressed and Steve lay in bed saying, 'I don't feel very well, I need to take the day off.'"

"He never takes a day off when he's ill?"

"Not unless he's dying."

"You thought it unusual?"

"Very! I said I would do the same. I could go in any time, you see."

"What did he say?"

"He got really mad, and that's when I got suspicious. Why was it so important for me to go to the office, and for him to stay home?"

"Eventually, he persuaded me to go. So I left, but halfway there I turned round and came home—he was really mad."

"You should have parked on the street and watched to see if he left or if Megan visited the house."

"I think in a way, I didn't want to catch him at it. What would I have done?"

"You were scared you would have to leave, and you had nowhere to go!"

"Exactly!"

"So what happened?"

"Nothing. Eventually, we stopped seeing them. But every so often I bring it up; I want him to come clean about it ... but he won't."

"What does he say?"

"That Megan has black hairs up her nose, that he could never go with a woman who has a hairy nose."

"How would he know unless he was really close up to her nose, or on top of her?"

"It's like a chasm between us."

"You mentioned prison before, what's that about?" The dark side scrutinizes every little wrinkle until there is nothing left but a smooth void.

The woman is still evasive on that subject, instead she says, "Two years ago he went to Dublin on business. One of the women was a friend of ours."

"Attractive?"

"No, but very bubbly, laughs a lot."

"And you think he screwed her?"

"He changed hotels while he was there. It seemed strange to do that."

"He said it was to save money."

"I didn't believe him."

"You don't believe anything he says."

"That's the problem."

"What makes you think he screwed her?"

"Nothing concrete. I know they walked along a cliff top together."

"He told you?"

"Yes. The thing is, we never see them anymore."

"That's not quite true, you went water skiing with them and you thought she was over-friendly with Steve."

"I'd forgotten that. It was a look she gave him. An *I know what's in your pants* kind of look. I think Steve wished he hadn't done anything with her..."

"Or maybe he still sees her!"

"Maybe."

"Maybe it's all in your head!" Into the silence, the dark side reminds the woman, "What about the thievery stuff?"

"One of the companies he worked for in England, before we came to the States, well, Steve was friends with the Director. He told Steve he was going through a really bad divorce, that he desperately needed money ... that the company had screwed him out of thousands of pounds. Steve felt sorry for him."

"Go on, before my blood petrifies with boredom."

"The director devised this plan to fiddle expenses and needed Steve's help."

"I assume Steve kept some of the money himself."

"No."

"What?? Why the hairball did he do it then!!"

"He felt sorry for the guy."

"And Steve never got a penny?"

"No ... thank God. I could never live with myself if he had."

"Were you involved in this deceit?"

"Steve told me about it, and I said no, he shouldn't do it. Then one day, I was looking through some stuff, and I couldn't believe my eyes."

"He'd been signing off expenses for stuff I know the director hadn't been on and the horrible thing was that he'd sworn to me that he hadn't done it."

"So if you had never found the expense copies, you would be none the wiser?"

"Right. I couldn't believe what a liar he was. He stood there in front of me, and swore that he hadn't done anything!"

"What did you do?"

"What could I do? Go to the company and tell them that my husband had helped an employee fiddle expenses!"

"Why did you stay with him? No let me put it a different way, why do you stay with him?"

"I love him."

"That's like loving a wife beater. Steve keeps lying to you and you keep on believing him—believing he will change."

"It does get harder. I feel sometimes, that I can't believe anything he says or does. It's the small things, the everyday things."

"Explain please."

"Well here's a good example. We send money to England for our pension, but we stopped because we had no money. Then when we finally did get some money, I asked Steve if we were up to date, he said, 'Yes', but I don't know whether to believe him or not."

"It's a big problem," says the dark side nastily. "Lying is a disease; once it takes hold ... it's almost impossible to stop—like being an alcoholic."

"I heard a radio program the other day that said alcoholism was not a disease!" The woman wished she had remembered the conversation now.

"Whatever." The dark side is not interested anyhow.

"I think he's really trying to be honest now, but I don't know," says the woman pathetically.

"You think other people sense that he lies."

"Yes, even though he's done it successfully for years, people can smell it."

"What can he do about the past? If he comes clean about everything, what's going to happen to his marriage? Would you leave him?" asks the dark side.

"No. In fact I would be over the moon if he could sit down and just be honest about his whole life—if he could tell me everything."

"That's dangerous," sniggers the dark side. "But interesting."

"He believes that helping that Director was a good and decent thing to do. That he needed it, that the company had it to spare, that he was doing a good deed! But it's nuts to think that way, how do we atone?"

"Why do you say 'we?' You weren't the one writing out false expense claims."

"If I had been stronger in the beginning, I could have stopped it. When Steve first mentioned it, I could have been so outraged that he would never have started."

"But you are not responsible."

"I have to take some of the responsibility."

"What happens now?" The dark side, as usual, digs to the core of the problem.

"That's just it, I don't know. On a spiritual level, I think the lies are killing him."

"Did you perform any kind of ritual to get rid of the karma?"

"Oh yes. I sat and chanted the mantra, 'OM NAMAH SHIVAYA' for over an hour, and visualized the problem disappearing. Then I submerged myself in a bath of very hot salt water and saw every aspect of the problem being washed away. Finally I got out, curled myself into a fetal position, surrounded myself in golden light and pictured things the way I wanted them to be. It was like being reborn."

"And did it work?"

"For me it did, but what about Steve?"

"Steve has to find his own method of cleansing. You can't do it for him."

"I can pray."

"It depends how you do it. If you feel pity, it's a judgment—which is no good."

"How should I pray then?"

"From your heart. Ask for forgiveness for him, and that he will find a way to cleanse himself."

"Do you think if Lucifer confessed, all would be forgiven?"

"Who cares?"

"Well, I'm here to tell you that it has happened."

"Lucifer has confessed?"

"Yep, there is no devil anymore, just the one in your head! You see, if Steve finds a way to cleanse himself, he's getting rid of the devil in his head. The problem is, he isn't fully aware it's in there. He's in that deep, deep river."

"What river?" asks the dark side.

"De-Nile!" answers the woman.

"Ha ha! It will be interesting to see what happens after he's read this. Have you ever considered the fact that he might not be lying? That he never did screw Megan?"

"Yes."

"What if he didn't?"

"You're right. I'm going to have faith that he didn't. Otherwise I'm acting the same as Sheila."

"Just a minute. I didn't tell you to have faith!" The dark side feels weakened. It has been far too helpful ... suckered into talking from a positive point of view. This is not right, not right at all!

Meanwhile, the woman is convincing herself to have faith in her husband. She picks up the old tattered copy of her father's Holy Bible, flips it open and reads, *the righteous, and the wise, and their works, are in the hand of God: no man knoweth either love or hatred by all that is before them. All things come alike to all: there is one event to the righteous, and to the wicked, to the good and to the clean.*

Without completely understanding why, the woman has faith that everything is in the hand of God. That she can stop worrying. That everything will come out perfectly in the end ... whatever that end may be.

MARATHON MAN

"Can you give me a healing tonight?"

"No!"

"Okay." Steve's quiet acceptance is like a bucket of ice water on her emotions; it sends the woman searching for a fresh kindling of words, "I'm not in the right frame of mind! I wouldn't do you any good! I don't think you should go anyway!"

"It's okay, I understand. I'm going to use your name tomorrow when I need strength, I'm going to call your name out over and over in my mind!"

The dark side reads her mind. "Most women would be proud, but all you think is, 'I never said he could use my name!' You really are a wonderful dirt bag!"

Steve, oblivious of the other conversation, sits back and reads to himself from the *Chicago Sun-Times*: *'The rock-solid foundation in place for the LaSalle Banks Chicago Marathon wasn't built overnight. When you've been in the valley, getting to the mountain is something that is done carefully and thoroughly. You make some sacrifices along the way, but you keep moving forward.'*

"I'm off to bed!" The woman closes the door on the word 'bed'. Angry that he is running the marathon.

Steve calls back, "I'll join you in a minute." His words hit the door and slide down like a jazz note at a Mozart recital.

Next morning the woman hears Steve wake before the alarm gets hysterical. She senses him slip from the bed thinking, *'I am not going to drive him to the marathon,'* and waits for him to tell her to get dressed.

Ten minutes go by; she hears him in the kitchen. Another ten, while he mixes a protein drink and takes vitamins. *'If he doesn't come and wake her soon, she won't have time to get dressed, even if she wants to!'*

At last he pads into the bedroom; she feigns sleep. He kisses her on the cheek, his lips feel soft and gentle on her sleepy skin. "Bye darling," he whispers. "I'll see you when I get back." He gives her hair a loving pat and leaves the bedroom.

The woman's body feels uncomfortable, like a cork being unscrewed from a hundred-year-old bottle of wine. Quickly her mind sorts through 46 years of experience and can't find one to match. In the gray pre-dawn, she projects how her morning will pass while Steve runs his marathon. All options look as miserable as a tethered dog on a frozen stoop.

Like a pre-tabbed bullet point, she leaps out of bed, goes to the window and bangs on the glass. Steve, sitting in the car with the engine running, figuring out the marathon route and the best place to park, is oblivious to her thumping and yelling.

She whips a towel round her naked body, dashes to the back door, covers six porch steps in two, runs to the car and shouts, "Steve, wait! I'll take you!" The window slides down as if Steve had been expecting her. "You had better be quick then."

The woman throws herself back in the house, screws feet and arms into sweats and bounds back to the car like a young whippet. "I couldn't let you go on your own," she says.

"I'm glad you're here," says Steve.

They ride in silence.

"But not for long with a motor mouth like you around." The dark side has watched the antics of the past hour and is disturbed by the woman's speedy recovery from what looked like a morning of deep depression.

"Shut up!" says the woman to her dark side. "I won't fall prey to your dreary ruminations." The woman thinks about the morning so far, and says to Steve, "I don't know what happens to me. Here I am, supposedly a swami priest, my husband asks me for a healing the night before his marathon, and I refuse! I don't know what to do about myself."

"You were worried about me. You didn't want me to run."

"True." The excuse rams into her brain like a log shooting the Grand Rapids. "You were really sick earlier this week. My guru says running saps the energy." She adds, unhelpfully, "Are you sure you feel okay to run 26 miles?"

"Twenty six POINT TWO!" says Steve, as if the *point two* mile is the difference between a fully organized marathon and a casual Sunday morning stroll. "I feel fine," he adds, "and if I feel bad at any time, I'll stop! I want to at least try it."

"Okay. You promise to stop if you feel ill or anything?"

"Promise—and if I don't finish," Steve falls silent for a moment, "I'll deal with that if it happens." The woman heads toward Columbus and Balbo. Grant Park is aswarm with runners moving east toward the lake.

"A veritable migration of dick heads," says the dark side. "People running like crazy to get back to the same point they started from."

The woman ignores the comment.

"Should I keep my pants on, or strip down to my shorts? What do you think?" Steve turns to the woman as if she has the consummate answer.

"I don't know," she answers.

"Is it very cold out?" he asks

"It's not hot."

"What's everyone else wearing?" They look at the conglomerate of runners wearing a veritable salmagundi of garments: hats, gloves, pants, jackets, shorts and t-shirts.

"Just a cotton-picking minute, dum-dum!" The dark side interrupts the woman's flow. "Why are you putting a word like 'salmagundi' in? Do you even know what it means, you insufferable clod?"

"It's a mixture or a medley!"

"It's a dish of chopped meat, eggs, etc. flavored with onions, anchovies, vinegar and oil," says the dark side darkly. "Just keep to the facts and nothing but the facts; stop trying to outsmart the reader." The dark side retreats, mumbling "stupid dunderhead" under its breath.

The woman double parks the car. In the chaos of 12,000 people trying to reach a single point at the same time, no one notices the misdemeanor. "I'll take my pants off and keep my jacket on. I can always tie it round my waist if I get too hot." Steve peels his running pants off to reveal two white legs sticking out of a pair of high cut running shorts. The legs look very vulnerable to the woman, so she tries to concentrate on something more substantial. She cannot find anything.

Steve turns to her and says, "It took me two hours to run 14 miles the other day, so I'm going to try and make it in four hours. We start at 7:45AM, which means I should finish around 11:45AM."

"Okay, I'll be back for you then. Good luck." They lean over and smack lips like the thin parchment kiss of a great grandparent. Steve gets out of the car and joins the throng of runners. She looks at his disappearing figure. His legs look almost too big now compared with other spindly frames. She pulls her eyes away, pretends that he will be fine and drives back along the Edens.

Showered and dressed, she takes her mind off Steve and the marathon by cooking a hearty meal for his return. Her nervousness clashes against the pots and pans until they are in mutinous uproar. With the finesse of a head-banger at a tea-party, she throws the meal together, tainting the food with unbalanced vibrations so that her digestive system reels at the thought of eating.

Shyam is asleep upstairs. "SHYAM! SHYAM!" She calls from the bottom of the stairs.

"Yeah." The voice sounds like it's been dredging the bottom of Lake Michigan for twelve hours.

"DO YOU WANT TO COME AND PICK UP DAD FROM THE MARATHON?"

"Huh?" Sixteen fathoms, with silt clinging to the vocal chords.

"I'M LEAVING IN TWENTY MINUTES!" shouts the woman thinking how nice it would be if she had been brought up not to shout round the house.

"Okay." Eight fathoms, but rising steadily.

"I'M A BASKET CASE!" The woman shouts back, but this time there is no reply.

"Nobody cares!" The dark side enjoys the woman's emotional state. Watching the various complex reactions play havoc with her mental and physical bodies is fun.

Ten minutes later Shyam says, "Got the camera?" He is dressed and ready to go.

"Yep!"

"Film?"

"Yep?"

"Let's go."

They park by surreptitiously moving a white painted railing aside and sneaking their car alongside the curb. The metallic, thermal sheets handed out at the finish line, flash silver across the shoulders of thousands of runners who have completed the run. Shyam and his mother push their way through yards of people paving the streets. Finally, they reach the bleachers where WBBM is providing live updates. The woman and Shyam force their way to a vantage point.

As far south as they can see, crowds line the route forming a land-locked isthmus; down the narrow passage in between, the heads of a thousand runners bob like corks blown forward on a wind tossed ocean.

"Do you think he's already finished?" asks Shyam.

"No. He's still out there." The woman acknowledges her female radar system.

A woman behind them shouts, "Go Terri, Training Go, Go, Go!" After a minute it becomes very annoying.

The announcer calls out, "Two minutes to finish under four hours." Five minutes later he reminds us, "Let's send a cheer to all the people still out there. Remember, they've been running for over four hours now, and it gets much harder the longer they run!"

Shyam looks far into the distance and shouts, "Come on dad, keep going, you're nearly home!"

The dark side sneaks in a thought, "Perhaps he's vomiting in a back alley. Perhaps he died from a heart attack!"

The woman sends positive thoughts to counter-balance her fears. 'Come on Steve, you can do it. Just a bit more and you'll be safe and home.'

"Go Terri, Training Go, Go, Go!" The voice is now a loud, cackling heckle, like the sound of chalk grating across dry slate.

'I wish you would Shut The Fuck Up!' thinks the woman alongside the forty other people in her immediate vicinity.

The people now bobbing to the finish line cover the gamut of human diversity: an old woman shuffles along, her feet swinging like pendulums. A man in his mid-forties pumps his arms like pistons. Two young men thrust hips, legs and torsos forward as if competing in a one hundred yard dash.

"Where is he?" shouts Shyam amid cheers as a young woman; her right leg, painfully distorted by a cramp, hobbles wretchedly to the finish. She is supported by a man serving as a human crutch.

"He'll be here soon," answers the woman.

"He won't!" answers the dark side. "You'll find him in the medical compound, dying from exhaustion." The woman ignores the voice.

At precisely 4:28PM the woman sees the figure she has known most of her life. "There he is!"

"Where? Where?" Shyam has the camera slung round his neck but does not know where to direct the lens.

"There, over there!" The woman pulls the camera toward her, half-garroting Shyam; she points and clicks. "Thanks mom!" says Shyam, rubbing his neck. "Where is he?"

"There!" The woman points to a figure in a white t-shirt, running shorts and blue jacket tied around the waist. "He looks great!"

"Dad! Dad!" Recognizing his son's voice above the rest of the crowd, Steve looks toward the bleachers and spots Shyam. His face lights up like a computer on Monday morning; he waves and points to the finish line as if to say, *'I'll see you there!'*

Like an assault team, they maneuver through jammed bleachers to the sea of human condition below. People create barriers in every direction. Couples stop dead in mid-stream; large groups form beaver dams, refusing to budge. Slow meanderers cause irritated bottle necks, fast paced hustlers jab and elbow their way as if on a presidential mission.

Slowly threading their way along the railings, they scan the inside of the finishing arena for their winner. Throngs of runners grab at water, Gatorade and bananas. "Where's he gone?" shouts Shyam above the noise and hubbub.

"Over there!" bellows the woman. "Leaning against the railing!"

At first sight, he looks fresh from a Saturday morning, six miler with the Lake Forest Running Club. "You look great!" shouts the woman across the barrier of railings.

"I feel great!" returns Steve. "I'll see you up there." Slowly he turns away from the finishing arena and walks to the public access. The pain in his legs is now obvious. "I could eat a horse," he says when he sees them. The woman pulls out a bag of bagels, grapes, raisins and nuts. "I'll take a bagel," says Steve, desperately trying to walk normally.

"Are you okay dad?" asks Shyam, noticing his hobbling gait.

"I can't feel my feet, but apart from that, I'm great!" laughs Steve.

"How was it, dad?"

"Fantastic."

"There were some real old people running!" says Shyam.

"I know," Steve chuckles, "this sixty-year-old man flew past me like a bat out of hell. I felt like tripping him up and smacking him one!" He takes a swig of water. "It was amazing. People took expensive running gear off and just left it at the side of the road!"

"Will they find it afterwards?"

"No way!" laughs Steve. "People swooped down and carried it off." He untied his jacket. "I'm amazed I kept this on. After a while my body knew where every bit of clothing was touching. It was like an itch, but I concentrated on feeling light and it passed."

"Did you hit the wall?" asks the woman.

"At about 18 miles, I thought I couldn't run any further."

"What did you do?"

The dark side rears its head. "You want to know if he used your name like he said he would. Don't worry dear, it's just your huge enormous ego needing its hourly stroke!"

"I repeated your name over and over in my mind. 'It gave me the strength to keep going to the next water place. They were set up every two or three miles along the route. Course it's impossible to actually drink any of it when you're running! I had water everywhere." Steve pretends to throw a cup of water over his face.

"What about going to the toilet?"

"They had portaloos! Some men kept running and just peed down their legs!"

"My God!"

"Some stopped," said Steve, defending the runners, "turned their back to pee, and went at the side of the road."

"What about the crowds?"

"Nobody cared. People were lined up the whole twenty-six point two miles. Some shouted, 'Go St. Aldus!' That's what it says across my t-shirt. Some people had their name written on their hat, so people shouted, 'Go Tim! Go Sharon! Go Bill!' Everyone was cheering. It was great."

At her next meditation class, the woman tells the group, "I was horrible to Steve over the weekend." She gives details about how she, a supposed healer, refused to help her husband prepare for his marathon.

"You were being a mom. You wanted to protect him," says one of the group.

"It wasn't right," says the woman. "I was being selfish."

"You were worried he might injure himself," says another.

"Not really! I remember Shyam saying once, 'Mom, I hate you worrying about me; it means you don't trust me to do a good job!' It clicked with me suddenly; worry means not having faith in someone's ability. Basically, I was telling Steve I didn't have faith he could run a marathon."

"They don't get it," says the dark side. "They think being a mom means being protective. If I were you, I would stop preaching."

"Besides, I'm not Steve's mom!" continues the woman. "He's already got a mom, he doesn't need his wife to be one. He wants me to support his decisions, not make him afraid."

"It was fine," says Steve. "I understood you were afraid for me."

"Well, it won't happen again," said the woman.

"Sure," answers the dark side.

Next morning, Steve walks through her room, on his way to the bathroom for a morning pee. His male appendages look cute and defenseless. She stops him and weighs them in her hand. "These seem heavy!"

"I need a pee, that's why."

"Why would that make them heavy?"

"Everything around them is heavy." He cups them as if they are on display at the Farmer's Market.

"Have your pee and I'll weigh them when you come back." She takes hold of them a few minutes later and is surprised they seem lighter. "It's amazing how little I know about your body," she says.

"I'm off for a short run," he says.

The woman sits at her computer and writes, "I love Steve more than I ever have in my life. For some reason, his running the marathon has made me look at him differently. He is my Marathon Man. He can do anything he sets his mind to."

"You just want to show him off!" says her dark side.

"I do," she says. "And it feels good. I love him so much, my heart could burst."

"Yeah, yeah, yea!" The voice of her dark side fades like a bullfrog at dawn.

"As if my heart could burst," she adds happily.

DEVIOUS DIVA

"Why are you here, when I'm not here?" asks Kate when the woman walks into the store where Kate works.

"What do you mean? she asks, knowing exactly what Kate means.

"Why are you here, when I'm not working?"

"You are working!"

"I'm not supposed to be working," says Kate.

"I just stopped by. I was shopping. I wanted to see what you had on sale." Words fluster round her mouth like heated popcorn.

"You thought she wouldn't be there," says her dark side. "You hoped you wouldn't see her."

"It's true," replies the woman. "I almost decided not to see Kate any more."

"Like most of your friendships, when the going gets tough, you get going." The dark side reminds her of broken friendships she has never bothered to mend. "Besides, Kate is a Capricorn!" says the dark side.

The woman is a Gemini and for some reason Capricorn females show up in her life as problems. The last Capricorn friend walked out of her life and never came back.

"Because you hurt her. You lied! Capricorn women neither forgive, nor forget; their revenge knows no statute of limitations, which is great from my point of view." The dark side fans the woman's discordant thoughts with fact or fiction.

The woman scans her astrology books for answers. Finally she goes to the kitchen, hunting for food. Two pink grapefruits catch her eye, she takes one, cuts it in half and saws round the edge to separate the white pulp from the fruit. She puts it into a bowl and carries it back to her writing room as if it holds the key to life.

As she digs a segment out, grapefruit juice spits across the keyboard. The segments displayed like a wheel, remind her of

the astrology wheel: twelve sun signs from Aries to Pisces; each
with its own characteristic and emotional element. "You know,"
she says to her dark side, "I always apply the worst aspects of
Gemini to myself: dual personality, fickle, restless, gossipy
mind."

"So you should, my devious little Diva!"

"I am those things, but Gemini is also the writing sign." The
woman quotes from Goswami Kriyananda's book, *The Wisdom
and Way of Astrology,* "From this sun-sign are born some of the
greatest talents and thoughts of the world, if Gemini's master
anything, they can go beyond the duality and be great souls."

"You, a great soul?" The dark side crouches, its sharp talons
prick her mind. "You are walking on dangerous ground. You
think you are god-like. You must make your ego small. "Its
voice wheezes in her ear. "Remember your short-comings. Tell
everyone about them. Be humble and full of guilt."

"No!" says the woman.

"What?" The dark side steps back.

"No!" she repeats. "I do have the God force within me." Her
mind is clear, like she's vacuumed it and discovered the Smith-
sonian Institute. "I can be a great soul if I overcome the negative
side of Gemini, and merge my two inner voices."

"It's impossible." The thought of harmonizing makes the dark
side feel sick.

The woman continues, "I realize why I don't get along with
Capricorn women."

"Why?" The dark side doesn't bother to suppress a yawn.

"I thought I was branded as a Gemini for life, but the fact is, I
have all twelve signs in my horoscope. I'm also Aries, Taurus,
Leo..."

"We get the picture."

"If I integrate the signs within me, understand what makes an
Aries fearless, courageous, headstrong and impatient, or a
Taurus, steadfast, enduring, stubborn and possessive. If I can
recognize each quality and element within myself, I won't be so
at odds with other people."

The dark side tries to side-track her. "Do something useful.
Go back to bed and masturbate!"

"The Capricorn urge is to live ambitiously, powerfully, and to attain higher social status, everything I hate. But it's within me: I have the urge to be powerful and make lots of money."

"So do it."

"I thought it was wrong to strive for distinction, honor and money."

"You write to create power," says the dark side. "You want people to whisper, 'she's the author of a best selling book, she must be important.'"

"I used to have that thought."

"You still do!"

"Yes." The woman swallows the word. Such a small confession for mankind, but such a large one inside her head. "With Kate, I recognize part of me that I haven't come to terms with."

"As usual you have managed to obscure your words," says the dark side.

"Okay, here it is in a nutshell."

"Form follows function and nuts have a myriad of complications intrinsic to their design!" says the dark side pompously.

"We're not talking ergonomics! I want to explain my thoughts that's all."

"Go for it, my hairy brained oaf!"

"Kate is a Capricorn. She has the urge to excel. She wants money, power and social status. I'm a Gemini, I have the urge to live communicatively, to be sensitive, strong-willed, gentle, kind and practical."

"Let's not forget, stubborn, sullen, furious and unyielding if angered." The dark side reminds her of the shortcomings.

"Within me is a Capricorn—weak because my sun doesn't shine on it, but it's still there. Kate reminds me of my Capricorn urges; I get angry because I feel powerless to activate them."

"Look further, you selfish idiot."

"What do you mean?"

"Capricorns lack confidence in their ability. Kate may see you as a confident person with the ability to take away her power."

The woman's head feels like a sump-pump working at a flash flood site; there is too much to take in. "Kate is a great person. I can learn from her instead of closing myself off."

"Let's get back on track. A difficult thing for a Gemini but please try. We left off when you were at the shop where Kate works."

"Ah yes. Kate says, 'I led the meditation at Ram's yoga class.' It's held at a local chapel. Immediately I think, bloody great! Ram asked me to help him teach his group, and now Kate is doing it."

"Did you say that?"

"No. I said, 'Wonderful.'"

"You lied."

"What else could I do?"

"Continue." The dark side enjoys its role as adjudicator.

"Kate says, 'It was hilarious, Ram's swami friend Prashant was there, he called me this morning, he wants to do a healing on me! It's as if the universe is giving me strength through other people. Like it knows I need help.'"

"But all you heard," says the dark side. "was that Prashant is giving Kate a healing and not you! You don't even know the man!"

"Yep." The woman accepts it with a bravado she does not feel. "I say 'great!' It's all I can manage."

"Because you're heart is a green monster, writhing in its own bile."

The woman agrees. "She tells me Prashant performed a ritual where he set fire to leaves in a big wok…"

"In the chapel?"

"It set off a fire alarm and the Lake Forest Fire Department arrived, but all the people in class were so spaced out from Kate's meditation, they wouldn't leave."

"How do you feel when you hear this story?"

"Okay. Then she says Ram called to remind her of tonight's meditation at his house."

"And you get pissed off, because he hasn't phoned to remind you, like he said he would."

"Exactly." The woman is surprised that her dark side is so affable.

"So you don't go to his house for meditation?"

"No, I do." The woman reads the words back on her screen. 'No, I do,' doesn't sound grammatically correct but it's her response. "When I get to Ram's everyone is there except Kate."

"What are they doing?"

"Playing drums, tambourines, rattles, chanting. Some people are dancing. It's great."

"How many people are in the room?"

"Not many; Ram, Mira, their daughter Geeta, George, Diane, Robert, Tim, Naomi, Claudine and Toinette." The woman counts on her fingers. "I join in the dancing, then we quiet down and sit in meditation, but I can't concentrate. I keep saying over and over in my head, *help me, please God help me.*"

"Help you what, dick wad?" The dark side hates it when she appeals to God for help.

"To unblock my heart. To heal the destructive forces within me. To stop wanting all power for myself."

"What happens?"

"At the end of the meditation, Ram comes over and kneads his fingers into the instep of my right foot."

"How is it?"

"I am amazed. It's like God answering my prayer. That I am worthy of attention."

"But you still need others to say you're worthy, it should come from within you. Tut, tut, tut!"

The woman ignores the voice and continues her story, "He holds my foot between the palms of his hand, and I feel pure love. Then he does the same with my left foot."

"Is it sexual?"

"No. Just love." The woman recalls the feeling and for a moment her body feels a glow like it is filled with sunshine. "He gently puts my foot down and leaves. I can't move, I just lay there on the floor, and George, a friend of mine who did Hatha Yoga Teacher's Training with me, says, 'What a beautiful angel you are.' Just like that, he calls me an angel."

"Lucifer is an angel. It doesn't mean anything." The dark side is relentless in keeping her ego down.

"George holds a tiny pair of cymbals low, above my head; and with a gently flick of his wrists, brings them together so a high pitched musical note enters both ears. The vibration fills my body. 'Follow the sound into your mind,' he says, 'clear all thoughts and allow your spirit to be filled with the glory of God.' It's like standing under a waterfall and having all my bad thoughts washed away—my heart opens like a flower."

"Then what?" The dark side has no time for flowers.

"He leaves me alone in the room with one white candle glowing on the altar. Tears spring into my eyes and I think about going upstairs and asking for help. I want to shout, 'Help me! Help me!'"

"I take it the others are in the kitchen sipping herbal tea and eating popcorn."

"Yes. I think about telling them of my bad feelings toward Kate, but something inside stops me."

"Well it isn't me!" The dark side encourages the emotionality of drama and gossip.

"I cry and sob until my heart opens even more."

"Does anyone come down to get you?"

"No. Eventually I dry my eyes and go to the kitchen. They look at me kind of funny. They can see I have been crying, but no one says a word. Claudine gives me some tea and cuts me a slice of apple cake. Ram is telling them about the yoga class."

"Kate," Ram says, "gave a wonderful meditation, then Prashant had everyone form a circle around Kate, myself and Mira." Ram chuckles at the memory. "He had everyone bow down and acknowledge us as high mystical teachers."

"My God!" said George in astonishment. "How awful."

"It was hilarious," says Ram laughing. "It was fun!"

"I'm not sure bowing down to other people is fun," says George.

"He was trying to get them to understand that we all have teachers," says Ram.

"It's true we all have teachers," says the dark side.

"The problem is, we fall in love with the teacher instead of the teachings," says the woman. "My guru warns that teachers are not infallible. That I should always question the teacher, including himself."

"So was it wrong for Prashant to get them to bow down?" asks the dark side.

"In a world of balance and harmony, I guess nothing is wrong and nothing is right, it just is," answers the woman, not sure if she really believes it. "When I saw Gurumayi in South Fallsburg, I bowed down to her and she blessed me. It felt odd to begin with."

"Why'd'ya do it?" asks the dark side.

"It's good for the ego to acknowledge great teachers," says the woman.

"You said this would be as simple as a nut shell. I'm more confused than before. What exactly is the point of this boring story?"

"When Kate told me the story of Prashant, she never mentioned he'd gotten everyone to bow to her and the other teachers. Kate was more interested in the funny aspects of the evening, than in blowing her own trumpet." The woman speculates for a moment. "Maybe we all swing in and out of our ego, and that's okay. After all, we need our ego to drive us forward into action."

"Praise be and hallelujah! If you didn't have an ego, I'd be out of a job," sneers the dark side.

"I sit at the table listening to them all talk, still wondering whether to tell them about my troubled feelings regarding Kate."

"I thought you had gotten over them, the massage, the crying, the herbal tea."

"Something in my body wants a dramatic scene with me playing the lead role. I can see it all—me crying, people putting their arms round me, feeling sorry for me!"

"Emotionality is great for dramatic roles," agrees the dark side.

"It's a struggle, because I get another feeling: the overwhelming urge to sit quietly and not say a word."

"How can a quiet voice have power?" smirks the dark side.

"It isn't a voice, it's a feeling," replies the woman. "I want to stay calm. I can manage not to speak my feelings, I will be rewarded by peace."

"Are you?"

"Yes. On the way home I stop at a gas station and buy a packet of Twix and a Mars bar."

"That's good, pile more fat on your already gross body."

"It's not for me, it's for Kate." The woman thinks about Kate for a moment. "She has a tough life, even though she's got pots of money."

"So?"

"She's a very dear friend to me."

The dark side splutters in disbelief, "give me a break, you lying, weasel-faced toad!"

"I mean it. I love her."

"So you give her the chocolate?"

"No. She's asleep. I write a note saying, Dear Kate, here's something to make your life a little sweeter. I sign my name with a smiley face, and leave it inside the screen door."

"I hate those smiley faces!"

"Next morning, the phone rings and it's Kate, 'Thanks for the candy,' she says, 'It was a really nice surprise when I opened the front door and saw it there with your note.'"

"What do you say?"

"I say, I'd really like you to come over and have dinner with us one night next week."

"And she says, 'no way, you greedy, power-hungry dick-head.'"

"Not at all. She says, she would love to."

"I'm going to throw up." The dark side makes puking noises.

"It's all I have to give, love and compassion."

"All we need is love, dah, da da, da dah, all we need is love," smirks the dark side.

The woman joins in, "dah, da da, da dah, all we need is love. Love. Love is all we need."

"Love is all we need." They finish together.

The woman sits back and looks at the leaves on the branches outside her writing room. Some are still green, but many are yellow and dying. Sunshine flickers through the blinds, lighting up her desk with mottled, dancing patterns of dark and light. She can't fathom it. Is the dark side changing? Were they actually singing a Beetle's song together?

"Can you help me?" asks the woman. But for once there is no reply. All is silent.

"Have you gone?" she asks.

The fingers on the keyboard find it hard to connect with the right letters. She types, *ljflkdj,* and then backspaces the letters away. She is totally confused. Her understanding is in chaos, yet far from feeling chaotic, she feels as if liberation is very close at hand.

"Are you ready for that healing?" she calls to Steve.

"Yes." He shouts back from the bedroom where he is reading.

"Are you prepared to do it my way? The candles, the music, the whole bit?"

"Yes mein-over-stumpen-führer," he says.

"You don't have to," she says.

"But I want to," says Steve. "I was only joking."

"Aha, the joking." The dark side looms up from out of a clear blue sky. "You still haven't got that bit, yet have you?"

"The joking?"

"Taking yourself too seriously."

"I'm working on it," replies the woman.

"Don't take too long. Life is not a dress rehearsal. This is it! The real thing! It's all you get."

"What about reincarnation?"

"What about it? If you have forgotten your past lives, what's the point?"

The woman cannot refute the logic. "Okay, if you help me work on my seriousness, help me with my ego, then perhaps I'll let you stay around."

"I'll let you know, scum-bag, snot-nosed reptilian-featured, ring-wormed piece of mucus."

The woman breaths a deep sigh. "How interesting," she says. "You really are a fascinating creature! Very, very interesting."

With that, she saves the text, turns the computer off and prepares to heal her joking husband.

Except that she doesn't. She tells him she needs a bath before she can heal him and says she will 'do' him after the bath. But when she finishes, she hears him watching TV and cannot bring herself to go near the 'box' to get him. Instead she goes to the bedroom and reads.

Thirty minutes later he walks in and says, "I thought you were going to give me a healing after your bath?"

"You were watching TV!" she answers.

"You could have come for me!"

"I didn't think you really wanted a healing!"

"Well I do. My back is killing me!"

"I'll do it after we get back from Chrissie's birthday party." The woman and Steve have been invited to a friend's birthday, and there is no time to do a healing before then and now.

When they get back from the party they settle down for the evening, the woman picks up some needle-point she is working on, and Steve switches on the TV. "Can I sit on that chair?" he asks.

"Why?"

"Because my back is more comfortable on that one."

"Okay!" But the woman is not okay. She is annoyed that his back is still hurting. That she has broken her word. "Would you like me to do something with your back now?" she asks grudgingly.

"Yes," says Steve.

"Lie on the floor then." He lies on his tummy and she sits across his buttocks so she can work on his back more easily. She presses deep circular movements with her thumbs, working them into and around the bones of his upper back. "Is this okay?" she asks.

"Ye ... sss," says Steve in a series of grunts and groans.

This, the woman realizes, is a massage rather than a healing.

"It's because you are afraid," says her dark side.

"Afraid of what?" she asks.

"Of what you will uncover."

"But Steve has already told me that he has nothing deep hidden within his psyche, nothing to hide." The woman recalls conversations in which Steve has denied any problems with his childhood.

"Maybe there is something even he doesn't know about!" urges the dark side.

"Well if there is, it should come out."

"So help him."

"Okay," she says. But the woman is unsure if she will, can, or even wishes to.

"You'd better," says the dark side. "I won't leave you alone until you do."

"I'm off to bed now," yawns the woman sleepily.

"So am I," says Steve. And off they go to bed, to bring the unconscious things into consciousness. To delve into the mysteries of their minds.

LAUGHING AT DARKNESS

She is looking to buy the house; it needs a lot of work, and in some places, urine has collected. In her dream, she buys the house, and now workmen are there, and the architect is showing her how badly built it is. "All the electric's run up the walls, when they should go down to the ground!"

"What about the rat?" Even in her dream, the dark side talks to her. "It looks like a ball of yellow fat half cooked in a pan of oil," it adds.

"It's in the roof of the house." In her dream, Steve has put rat bait up there, but the rat is living off it!"

"That must symbolize in your mind that Steve is feeding or fueling bad things!" says the dark side. "Which is probably part of the reason you don't want to give him a healing."

"The architect and the workmen stand round the toilet laughing. "It's been designed for the shit to stay here forever," says the architect. "But we can fix that."

In her dream, the house gets remodeled easily and with the best materials. Walls are built, sky lights put in, and a Jacuzzi sunk into the bathroom. More toilets are built, and everything becomes more and more beautiful. Then the bills start coming in. "How are we going to pay these?" the woman asks Steve in her dream.

"Don't worry, we'll get the money somehow!" he answers. So the dream continues with the workmen doing all kinds of wonderful things to the house, while the woman, even though she no longer expresses it, still worries about the money.

"What about the radio show?" says the dark side. "When the architect invites a group of gospel singers to entertain them, but they turn into sluts and floozies!"

"Steve goes up to one of them," says the woman, "and he asks her out even though he knows I am watching!"

150

"He doesn't care anymore. He wants rid of you," says the dark side.

"We end the relationship," the woman adds.

"You get worried about how to earn a living on your own."

"I become a sales person, until I get back on my feet."

"Is that how the dream ends?"

"Yes. Steve and I split, and I earn my own living," says the woman.

"You obviously still don't trust him." Her dark side interprets the dream for her. "You want to be independent and earn your own living." The woman lets her dark side continue. "You don't trust Steve to get the money for the home renovations. You don't trust him with other women, and basically, you want 'out' of the relationship. So why don't you?"

"Divorce him? There's no point," replies the woman.

"Why not?"

"I love him, and I like being with him."

"Why?" The dark side does not believe the woman.

"Because I know Steve. I would rather work on myself within this relationship, heal my feelings, my sense of trust. If I don't they will just rise up again with the next man I meet."

"What about the money?"

"We're starting to get some big contracts coming in. Money is beginning to flow again. I know we're going to be okay."

"But is okay enough? You have big debts to pay. The IRS will not wait forever."

"I know that," says the woman. "We'll pay them. By the middle of next year, all our debts will be paid, and we will have begun work on the house."

"That's a very big statement," says the dark side doubtfully.

"I feel it to be true," says the woman. "If everything begins with a thought, I will have…" The woman thinks of the things she wants to create. "Lots of money. Be a joy-filled healer. Earn my living writing and giving workshops. Be healthy, slim and fit. Have faith and trust in myself. Have all my family healthy and happy. Have them understand their God-given purpose in life…"

"Okay, okay that's enough!" says the dark side. "You are supposed to focus on one thing."

"Says who?" asks the woman.

"Says me."

"I override your limited vision," says the woman. "I have to be consciously aware of everything I want to create in my life because I am creating my future right now in this very moment."

"That's stupid," says the dark side sulkily.

"If we are supposed to live in the moment," says the woman, pausing for effect, "and our lives are made up of many moments..."

"Yes, yes, yes!" The dark side wants to speed up.

"And we create each of those moments."

"Yes, yes!"

"What we thought of in the past creates the moment we live today and our future tomorrow's!"

"What's your point, you old wind-bag?"

"If we think failure, that's what will happen!"

"So?"

"I have to think of everything I want to happen and see it coming true. But then, and here's the difficult part, I have to let go of it."

"Why let go?"

"Because if I hold on to it, I can't enjoy the moment I am in," says the woman. "If I hold on to my dreams, I become dissatisfied they are not happening now, and I create a dissatisfied future."

"It sounds very complicated."

"Not really. If I dream of everything I want in my life. Then let the dream go. Live in the moment as if the dream is a reality, and know I am creating my future in every moment of my life. If I want joy, I have to live joy!"

"What about me?"

"What about you?" asks the woman.

"Where do I fit in?"

"You are my dark side."

"Am I part of your dream?"

"In a way," says the woman, afraid of having her dark side with her forever.

"You're afraid of me." The dark side knows her fears.

"Yes."

"Why? What can I possibly do?"

"Make me do things I don't want to do."

"How?"

"If you are involved in my thoughts, you will become part of my creation."

"So you want to kill me off?"

"I want to be friends with you."

"I've already told you! It's impossible. I am a dark side. I don't want to be friends with the light—it takes too much energy."

"What do you suggest then?"

"Acknowledge me from time to time and let me do my business."

"What is your business?"

"To be dark."

"What's the point?"

"So you can see the light."

"I can do that without you."

"You can't see light if there is no dark—it's impossible."

"My brain hurts," says the woman, laughing.

"So does mine," agrees the dark side.

"You see. We are beginning to understand one another," says the woman at the outer edges of understanding.

"I'm not sure about that," says the dark side, unwilling to relinquish control. "If I expose everything about myself and there is nothing left, what will happen to me?"

"Nothing."

"So I will become nothing?"

"Right."

"I will cease to exist? Is that what you're telling me?"

"No. You will still exist. Except you will exist as nothing."

"I don't get it!"

"You have a past, right?"

"Yes."

"And you have a future, right?"

"Yes."

"And in between those two things, there is nothing, right?"

"I'm not sure."

"It's the space in between breaths. You breathe in, you breathe out and there is a space in between where there is no breath. It doesn't mean you have stopped breathing, but the space of no breath, is the moment of stillness between past and future. It's the reality."

"Why do you make everything so damn confusing?"

"Because it is too simple to be anything else," laughs the woman, wishing she could make it even simpler. "If you didn't breathe out, you couldn't breathe in. If you didn't have a past, you couldn't have a future. The moment in between the past and the future is where you live life. The stillness between the outgoing breath and the incoming breath is where you connect with God."

"Oh great, bring God into it now and really confuse the issue," snarls the dark side.

"It's mystical. It's harmonious and inharmonious. It's good and bad. It's light and dark. The space in between, the nothingness..."

"Stop!" screams the dark side. "I can't stand anymore of your stupid psychology. Go, work, leave me in peace, allow me to palliate."

"Calm down, I'm going!" Unusual, thinks the woman. The dark side wants me to shut up, usually it's the other way round. She laughs to herself, switches off the computer and begins to mail out invoices.

Everyone Is A Purpose

"You're always talking about dad's ego." Shyam and his mother are sitting in the Egg Harbor having breakfast. "Dad has the least ego of anyone I know! I think that's the reason other people rip on him so much!" He continues, "It's because they hear you rip on him, so they think it's okay for them to do it!"

"You're right!" says the woman thinking of all the times she has exposed Steve's ego in public. "I do that don't I?"

"Yes mom, you do."

"So it's really my ego I see, not his!"

"Could be." Shyam does not want to be too hard on his mom, but he is glad she can see an aspect of herself that has been cloaked for so long.

"When I talk divorce, it's really me I want to get away from?" The woman says this more to herself than to Shyam. "Dad wants me to give him a healing, but I don't want to."

"What!!" Shyam looks up from his 'Sunny Oatmeal!' "I can't believe you would do that."

"I can't believe I would either!" The woman shakes her head at the surprising things she does. "I'm afraid of what I might dig up if I delve too far into his psyche!"

"Then you have to do it!" Shyam turns a pair of *shark-like* eyes on his mother: penetrating orbs of black light focus with deadly intent. "Dad is the most open person I know. He has no ego. He's just asking for a healing on his back!" Shyam blinks and shakes his head. "I don't know, mom!"

"Okay, I'll do it." From a dim, distant corner of her mind a thought comes into her consciousness. It's a thought she has suppressed many times. "I'm scared to do a healing on Steve because I'm afraid of losing control!"

"Way to go mom!" Shyam puts his orange juice down with a thwack that creates monster waves in the glass.

"When I do a healing, I have no idea what's going to happen. We could end up anywhere!"

"So?" Shyam does not understand his mom's problem.

"If dad is in control of where we go, I have to give up control of him."

"So?"

"Then I have to give up control of myself!"

"So?"

"So!" The mother sits in silent confusion.

Later, at home, the dark side returns to the problem.

"Remember the astrology book, what it said about the Gemini?" The dark side prods her memory. "The bit about ego-ambition."

"No," says the woman.

"Gemini women have ego-ambition. They are competitive with men in the business world!"

"And?" The woman holds up her hands in a 'get to the point' type gesture.

"You work with Steve in the business world and are in constant competition with him."

"How can I stop?"

"Stop being in the business world with him."

"I want to be independent."

"Good."

The woman does not feel good however. "I'd be running away again; I want to stop my competitiveness."

"That might happen when you're dead."

The word 'PEACE' floats across her mind like a wave on the ocean. It suggests that the answers are within, that she should meditate. Without another thought, the woman sits cross-legged on the floor, turns her head to the left and exhales twice over her left shoulder. 'The resurrection breath!' she thinks. 'My next inward breath will be symbolic of my rebirth!'

She breaths in a long, steady, stream visualizing her breath circulating icy cold up the front of her spine over the top of her head and descending hot with the out-breath down the outside of her spine to rest at the base, where she starts the whole process again.

Fifteen minutes later she sits down at the keyboard. The telephone rings, "Hi darling!" It's Steve. "How are you?"

"Great, how are you?"

"I've just had a brilliant call. Met with the president of this company, he loves everything, and we're going to do business, they want three, two-day programs on Customer Satisfaction!"

"Fabulous. How much do we get?"

"Twelve thousand!"

"Wonderful."

"I'll be home for lunch—will you?"

"Yes. I've got soup ... and lots of other wonderful things to eat," she adds quickly, thinking: 'I must get some Foccacio Bread and hummus.'

"I'll see you around twelve then."

"Great. I love you."

"Love you too."

The phone clicks dead, she walks to the kitchen for a glass of water. Millie, the dog is lying on her bed almost under the kitchen table. It's the place she first sought as a puppy, frightened of her new surroundings. She was too young when she left her mother, so small she couldn't even climb down the kitchen step to go outside.

"Hi little Millie." The woman kneels beside her dog and kisses the top of her head. Millie's tail wags sleepily, too comfortable to make a big fuss. "Is it nice being a doggy in our home?" she asks, remembering what Shyam told her the night before when she got annoyed with Millie for sleeping on her bed.

"Mom, you gotta think of Millie as a special person, you tell them to do something and at the time they do it, but two hours later they've forgotten everything you said!"

The woman strokes her dog's velvet fur and allows her mind to wander back to last Saturday evening, the Chicago Emmy Awards. She was helping with the production, nothing too strenuous, assisting the presenters, making sure they were backstage on time. It was like a boutique of egos; some, the ones born into 'the lucky sperm club,' sat next to the stage. The unlucky sperm club, sat in the over-spill room down the hallway!

"I've paid the same as everyone else!" cries one over-spill lady whose body is tightly pinned in with sequins. "I refuse to eat in that little room!" Unfortunately, nobody cares whether she refuses or not, and true to the very nature of frustration, she finds herself seated with the very people she does not want to be seated with. "We need a host for a new show we're putting together," she says to the only other person at the table with possible star quality.

There follows a long and boring 'pecking order' discourse during which, both ladies determine not to look at the unknowns sitting at their table, God forbid, they take it as an invitation to join in.

The woman turns to Ray, her friend, and says, "I'm having these awful thoughts."

"About what?" he asks.

"That I'm here with all these film people, script writers and such, and I should be talking with them, networking, that kind of thing."

"Then why don't you?"

"It seems so scuzz ballish!"

"You are here for a purpose, just like it says in the *Celestine Prophecy*," he adds with a smile.

The woman turns to the lady on her right and is surprised to find warm friendly eyes. She will never have judgments again, she thinks.

"Until the next time!" says the dark side under its breath.

"Hi, did I hear you say you've written a film script?"

"Yes. Hi, I'm Trudy, I've just come back from a three month stint in Hollywood."

"Wonderful, what were you doing there?"

The conversation twists through the peaks and valleys of social decorum and finally ends up with the woman saying, "How did you get started in this?"

"I use to write scripts for corporations, then I took classes on screenplay writing and entered the 'Columbus Screenplay Discovery Awards.' I won first prize and everything changed."

"I think of entering competitions; they have lots in the *Writer's Market*, but I never do; maybe I should!"

"Absolutely you should!" replies the stranger who has more faith in the woman's unknown talent than she herself.

"I will!"

"In about twenty years time when you're too old to get any satisfaction!" says the dark side.

The woman is called back stage and she never sees Trudy again, but later she says to her friend Ray, "Thanks for telling me that everyone I bump into has a special message for me. I was reminded to enter writing contests, that I should never give up!"

"Thank you," says Ray with a twinkle.

HEALING CHUBBIES

"Lie on the blanket." Gentle tones soften the directive. "Put your arms by your side and uncross your legs."

Steve relaxes, glad to be given instructions on how to heal his body. The woman's writing room which also serves as her healing place, is totally transformed. A soft, knotty pine desk holds a computer gazed down upon, by three angels perched high on a lintel above the window. A larger angel blows a trumpet across the CD player, and in the corner a two foot round table serves as an altar for sacred objects, each with its own memory: an eagle feather gifted to her on her vision quest, a wooden Confucius, brought back by Steve's grandfather from a far-off sea trip long ago. Two African Good Luck figures, from Silva, and a small crystal chest from Shyam.

The woman places her warm hands on Steve's temples. The oil on her hands smells like golden buttercups smiling into the sun. "Dear God, bless this space and open us to the higher forces of healing powers. Allow Steve to understand the pain in his back and remove the root cause of his suffering. Thank you." She sits in silence with her hands still on her husband's face. After a while she says, "Take three deep breaths. Breathe out any negativity, thoughts or judgments. Allow each breath to become a renewal of your mind, body and spirit. Allow all pain to become so heavy that you can no longer hold on to it. See it fall away from your body and be transformed into white light, so that it becomes positive strength within the universe."

The woman continues to relax him, until Steve feels unable to lift a finger. She moves her hands over his body in special Reike healing positions, and as she does, she probes and questions his deeper consciousness. "Take your mind back to the first time you ever felt any pain."

"I fell off my bike."

"Why?"

"It was too big for me and I was showing off."
"Where did you take the pain?"
"To my mother."
"How does she look to you?"
"Concerned, but I know everything will be okay."
"Do you feel comfortable with how you dealt with the pain?"
"Yes."
"Take your mind back to the next time you felt pain." The woman continues asking the questions until Steve has brought up all the painful events he remembers in his life. "Think about all these events and tell me what they have in common?"
"I was doing something stupid at the time."
"Take your mind back to last week, when you hurt your back. What are you doing?"
"Taking a bag of leaves to the garbage."
"How are you dressed?"
"In business clothes."
"What does the bag look like?"
"Dirty."
"See yourself in the business clothes together with the bag of leaves." The woman waits for the visualization to take place. "Do they belong in the same picture?"
"No."
"What should you be wearing?"
"Sweats."
"How do you maneuver the bag? Do you push or pull it?"
"Push it."
"Now visualize yourself at business. Do you push for new business or pull it in?"
"I push it."
"See yourself pulling it instead and tell me how that feels."
"It has more momentum—I can pull it more easily."
"Take your mind back to the garbage. You are dressed in your business suit, pushing a dirty, bag of heavy leaves to the garbage and you hurt your back. Why you didn't wait for a better time?"
"I wanted to surprise you."
"How long have the leaves been there?"
"About four weeks!"
"Why couldn't you wait?"

"I wanted to get it done!" The woman feels Steve's uncomfortableness.

"Did you have enough time to do the job before driving to your business meeting?"

"Yes."

"And if the bag of leaves had burst, would you have had time to change?"

"I would have been late."

"Seeing the bag of leaves now, would you still push it to the garbage if you were dressed in business clothes?"

"No."

"Steve, this is what I see." She doesn't wait for affirmation but continues. "There is a time and a place for everything. When you are dressed for business, focus on business. Detach yourself from me and any other distractions. Focus on yourself and what you need to do to pull in the business. Do the appropriate thing at the appropriate time. Read in a reading chair, sleep in a bed, eat at a table. Does that make sense?"

"Yes."

The woman moves to Steve's pain which is under his left shoulder blade. She puts her hands there and says, "Is the pain pushing or pulling at you?"

"Pushing."

"Visualize the shoulder being pulled back into place. Can you do that?"

"Yes."

"I'll help you." The woman gently massages the area, kneading the shoulder to aid Steve's inner visualization. After about ten minutes, she says, "How does it feel now?"

"Great."

"I want to ask you something that maybe I shouldn't ask."

The dark side butts in, "Don't ask personal questions when you're healing." It prefers her to keep all anxieties hidden.

"Go ahead," says Steve calmly.

"Who was the last woman you ever had an affair with?"

"The one in Bristol. fifteen years ago."

"Are you sure?"

"Of course I'm sure."

"Then why do I have these feelings of jealousy?"

"You don't trust me."

"But I have a problem. It's about my book! It's written as if you are still unfaithful, and I keep expecting you to come clean. My readers expect you to come clean! Why can't you just say you did what I accuse you of, then I can write it down!"

"But I haven't done anything!"

"Oh God. What do I write then?"

"I don't know. I didn't do anything."

"But it sounds like you did!"

"That's because it's in your head!"

The woman heaves a deep sigh. "Are you sure?" she asks.

"May the Lord shoot his hand through that window and pluck me up by the Testes! I didn't do anything!"

The woman laughs, and for the first time, really believes him. "Let's say an affirmation together. Repeat these words after me." The woman reads a few words at a time, allowing Steve to say them after her: *"The forgiving Love ... of Life ... washes clean the pains ... of the past ... and I am comforted. All things are forgiven ... and Love and Goodness ... are permeating all ... the facets of my life. Old things ... are passing away ... and I am renewed. I am a renewed soul ... in life."*

The woman repeats it twice again *sotto voce*. Then, standing with her hands above Steve's head, she sweeps them three times down to the bottom of his feet. She smoothes an invisible blanket over him with her hands, and visualizes him in a blaze of white light. "Okay, you're done!"

The woman sits at his side and waits for him to move. He begins to wriggle his shoulder looking for the pain. "It's amazing," he says.

"Don't look for it!" says the woman.

"Right!" he says, continuing to make small circular movements of his arm.

"I can't believe it," he murmurs. "It's gone!"

"Believe it," says the woman softly but firmly. "Just let it be now. Forget it!"

The woman goes to the bathroom to relieve herself and wash her hands; a ritual she always performs after a healing. She returns to give Steve a hug and feels his hardness with surprise. "You've got a chubby!" she laughs.

"It started during the healing." He looks down at her with fun in his eyes. "I had to restrain myself from putting my hand up your skirt."

"Ugh!" The woman's face screws itself inward toward her nose. "That's awful."

"Why?"

"Because while I was giving you a healing, all you were thinking about was sex!"

"I couldn't help it. When you relaxed me, I felt warm and safe, it just happened."

"I'm sorry, but I can't do anything about it now. I'm just not in the right space to make love."

"That's okay," Steve allows no disappointment to show. He, as usual, is very sensitive to his wife's feelings.

"Do you think other men get sexual when they come for a healing?" asks the woman, thinking about all the men she gives healings to.

"Maybe," says Steve.

"Oh My God!" Her face screws up again. "It's disgusting!"

"It's hilarious!" The dark side giggles at the thought. "There you are, all saintly and wise, surrounded by chubbie's and hard-on's."

"It probably happened to you, because you're my husband."

"Could be," says Steve.

"Don't you mind?" asks the woman.

"I feel great; if you do the same for other people, then it's wonderful."

The woman looks at his face, his eyes are wide and round with understanding, his nose almost too big, overshadows his mouth. His skin, a little wrinkled now, is baggy, like an old elephant. She looks at his features and feels an overwhelming wave of love rise up within her. This is her man, her mate, her lover. "Do you want to make love?"

"What do you think?" he says pointing to his groin, stiff and waiting.

"Let's do it then." She begins to undress. "I want to go under the bedclothes, where it's warm."

"He shouldn't be on top," warns the dark side. "The pressure on his arms will make his shoulder go out again."

The woman ignores the voice. Afterwards, when they are lying in each other's arms, she says, "Does your shoulder hurt again?"

"A little bit," says Steve. "But it's okay."

"Just visualize it pulling into place again." She gently reaches and massages his shoulder blade. "Imagine a green light penetrating your whole heart region," she says. "Allow it to circulate in a clockwise direction, like a CD of light, a plate of green energy spinning and opening up the space."

"It feels better," says Steve, drifting off to sleep.

"I feel better," says the woman. They slumber for 20 minutes. Each dreaming a conversation with themselves, a dialogue of symbols and images connecting the unconscious and conscious levels of their mind. "I only have two more chapters to go," she murmurs when she wakes.

"Then on to your next one," says Steve.

"I'm not sure," says the woman. "I want to help you in the business, there's a lot of work to do."

"True," says Steve. "But you must make time for your writing, it's too important to let drop."

"I do have the next title," says the woman.

"Oh yes?"

"The diary of Jesus' wife."

"Ah yes, I'd forgotten that."

"It'll be great," says the woman, smiling. Her life is as full and bountiful as it has ever been. She feels new places of happiness opening up inside her, as if the dark side, no longer crouching in corners, is just hanging around waiting to be summoned.

"Or not, as the case may be." The dark side is bored with the way it is being handled. It doesn't like to be dismissed so easily, it wants to think up some trouble. "Have you called for your colonic appointment yet?"

"No, but I will this morning."

"If you do that, then I will have great respect for you," says the dark side.

"You will?" asks the woman, surprised that a dark side could have respect for its host.

"I said it didn't I?" mumbles the dark side.

"Maybe we can be friends after all?"

"OVER MY DEAD BODY!" screeches the dark side.

"Don't worry, I don't kill things, even you." But still, with only two chapters to go, the woman is getting more and more worried about how the conflict will end. There must be a resolution, but as yet, it is very unclear.

CHOCOLATE OR HAPPINESS

The south door to the chapel is locked. Through the stained-glass window she sees chairs which are usually cleared to the side on yoga nights. She wonders if it has been canceled, but the soft glow from inside indicates life.

Walking through wet grass that reminds her of camping, she reaches a side door; it too is locked. She looks upwards, above the five foot walls, to an open archway with pillars connecting the chapel to the main building. She skirts round it, feeling clandestine and sneaky. She comes to a small opening and squeezes through.

Dead leaves scrape across the rain-soaked flagstones making them slippery like frog-skin. She enters through the north-facing door, and sees the silhouette of Ram and a woman embracing at the far end of the chapel. Her heart closes tightly as if encased in lead.

Feeling like a spy, caught but not yet sentenced, she sits quietly at the back of the chapel. 'It must be past 7:30PM, other people should be here!' she thinks.

"Why don't you go up to them and say how embarrassed you feel," whispers the dark side.

"It doesn't seem right."

"Why not? Yoga is supposed to free you from embarrassment; Ram is the teacher, tell him how you feel!" The dark side presses her to act.

"I don't want to disturb them." Low moaning sounds reach her.

"They're making out!" gasps the dark side, emulating as much horror as it can.

"I don't think so. They know I'm here, and we're in a chapel, for God's sake!"

"They don't care!"

"I'm going to sit and wait," determines the woman. "I am not going to do my usual; open my mouth or act without thinking."

"Have it your way," says the dark side, disappointed. "But, your future looks very boring if you handle things this way."

"I don't mind," says the woman, taking off her shoes and socks and placing them underneath a chair. Ram looks up toward the back of the chapel and waves her forward. Slowly she makes her way up the center isle until she reaches the couple. "Hi," she says softly.

"Hi." They both look up and smile.

"Hi!" says a fourth voice. She glances to her right and sees a purple yoga mat with a woman stretched along it. Looking closer, she is surprised to see Kate!

"Hi," she says, wondering if the three of them are in some secret ritual.

"Exactly!" says her dark side. "The three of them meet before yoga class to work on each other, and they haven't invited you!" The dark side reaches into itself to manufacture more bile. "It shows they don't consider you much of a teacher, or much of anything really."

The woman fights with her emotions. She does not want to feel jealous. She does not want to feel hatred or anger. She feels a wave of peace and breathes it in. The windows of the chapel read, *My peace I give unto you. Continue ye in my love.* "Have you been here long?" she asks Kate as they hug.

"I just got here."

"I gave Steve a great healing today," says the woman.

"Braggart!" says the dark side.

"What did you do?" asks Kate, interested.

"It's hard to explain, I used my intuition," the woman explains.

"That's the best way," says Kate, smiling. "Perhaps you could give me a healing after I have my knee surgery on Wednesday?"

"Of course. I'd love to." The woman thinks it strange Kate asking her for a healing. She had assumed Kate would think her unworthy.

"That's because you don't think you're worthy," says the dark side. "And of course, you're not!" it adds nastily.

Meanwhile, Ram and Gail are hugging. "Thanks for the healing," says Ram. "It's really helped my back."

"Any time," murmurs Gail warmly.

"What a load of bullshit," splutters the dark side angrily. "Hot, quivering thighs, that's what all this healing is about, sex and lust!"

"Oh my!" says the woman. "We really are getting angry, aren't we?"

"You should have taken action!"

"When?"

"When you saw Ram and Gail together."

"But I would have made a fool of myself; they were just giving each other a healing."

"It's no good if you don't get emotional," cries the dark side. "I can't exist without emotion. You're killing me!!!"

"I thought you said at the beginning of the book that you couldn't be killed, that you would just seek another human being to play with."

"I lied. I have to stay with you. It was a lot of bravado."

"Listen, I'm not killing you. I'm a peaceful person, but if you stay, you have to accept my rules."

"Never."

"You don't even know what they are!"

"I don't care, I will never accept."

"Have it your way."

The dark side slinks away feeling undernourished. It feeds off dark emotions and if the woman refuses to have them, what will happen? It determines to find a way to exist; it cannot die, it must live on.

At the end of the yoga class, Prashant enters the chapel and walks toward Ram. As he passes Kate he whispers, "I'm going to save your sorry ass!" To the rest of the group he says, "I am going to show you a very important posture. First you kneel down and sit on your heels. Rest your elbows and forearms on the floor in front of you. Slide them along until your forehead touches the floor. Do this toward your teacher, Ram. Send him your blessings and feel his blessings come toward you. Soak them up."

The woman thinks of the incongruity of the situation, Lake Forest, place of prosperity and wealth. The chapel, place of Christian worship. Prashant, Swami from India with long black hair tied in a pony tail. Adults prostrate on the floor like pilgrims.

"We are going to do a letting-go ritual. Ten minutes of shaking your body. Ten minutes jumping up and down. Ten minutes getting rid of all your anger and desires. And a final ten minutes, dancing in celebration." Prashant looks around the group. "Are you ready?"

"Yes!"

"Take a five minute break, then we'll start." During the break, Prashant arranges seven cushions on the floor. At one end of the chapel he puts a baseball bat, and at the other end a knife.

A student half jokes, "I hope we're not going to perform a blood ritual!"

The mention of blood ritual brings the dark side back to life, "What's going on?" it asks.

"Nothing," says the woman. "You might want to stick around though, we're going to get rid of a lot of anger, you could do with losing some."

"Never!" says the dark side slinking away again.

"Right!" Prashant's voice is loud through the microphone; the fast beat music even louder. "Shake!" he shouts at the group. "Come on, shake from your pelvis. Shake your groin. MOVE IT!!"

The woman shakes her head, arms, and legs. It is harder than it seems. She looks furtively round. Some people are shaking more than her, some less. "Close your eyes and SHAKE!!" screams Prashant, walking round the room. "COME ON!! SHAKE YOUR BODY!!"

After ten minutes of shaking, the music changes and a deep breathing sound is heard. The woman feels her breath, deep, and low, "HAH! HAH! HAH!" The sound is pushed out of her body every time she jumps.

"JUMP WITH YOUR HEELS ON THE FLOOR!" screams Prashant.

"You think you are rather good, don't you?" The dark side finds it impossible not to take part in the ceremony. "You think Prashant thinks you're good. That he recognizes a fellow swami!"

The woman ignores the voice and continues jumping up and down, stamping her heels into the carpet, "Hah! Hah! Hah!"

Each connection with the floor forces another 'Hah' breath out of her body.

"You think Prashant is aware of your strength, that he wants to meet you and tell you how wonderful your spirit, your soul, is."

Another ten minutes go by and the music changes again. It is still loud, still fast, but there are more instruments playing. "BEAT THE GROUND!" GET RID OF YOUR ANGER!" Prashant gets hold of the knife and stabs the cushion, demonstrating how to use it.

"This is what we did in Mystery School!" calls Kate to the woman.

"We did the same at the Intensive," replies the woman.

"Determined not to be outdone!" screams the dark side.

The woman goes to the far end of the chapel, picks up the baseball bat and beats the cushion. She tries to feel anger, hatred, but all she can feel is a deep joy. She lifts the baseball bat high above her head and brings it down hard, slamming into the cushion. Again and again she thrashes the cushion until she can lift no more. Then she lies down and flails the ground with her feet and hands as if she is a two-year old having a tantrum. It feels good to let everything out.

"But you're not letting everything out," shouts her dark side. "Listen to the other people, they are screaming names."

"I don't have any name to scream. I don't have the hate inside me anymore."

"Bullshit!" screams the dark side. "What about me?"

"I don't hate you!" The woman picks up the knife and stabs at the cushion, tearing at the warp and weft with each thrust. She feels a bubble of laughter rise up and lets it escape in a whoop of freedom.

Finally, the music changes to a medium beat with voices singing in celebration. "CELEBRATE! DANCE! KEEP YOUR EYES CLOSED AND CELEBRATE!!" shouts Prashant.

Her hands move like snakes and she remembers Steve years ago, laughing at the way she danced; now she laughs at herself too as she moves her body into strange shapes, twisting in and out of the space like an oriental belly dancer.

"Oh yeah! You're still thinking about how good you look. How Prashant must be noticing you. That he thinks everyone in the group should be like you." The dark side is relentless in its pursuit of the ego.

"You are right, I do have those ego thoughts; thank you for making me aware of them."

'Peace,' she thinks, 'peace!'

The woman dances and for brief moments loses herself in the dancing. Forgets to think about keeping her eyes closed. She sways, she leaps, she knocks into someone.

"Hey, this is my space!" It is Kate, but the woman just moves away. Floating to another space, peaceful, gentle and soft.

"How do you feel?" asks Prashant as the music stops and everyone stands still.

"Wonderful," they cry out.

"Great!" says Prashant and points to Ram, a young student and an older woman. "You, you and you, stand in the middle. Everyone else come round and make a circle. Bow to your teachers."

The woman gets on her knees and drops her forehead to the floor.

"I don't know whether you know it or not, but these three people kept the space open for all of you," Prashant says. "These are your teachers. Bless them and receive blessings from them."

"You are pissed!" chuckles the dark side. "You thought you would be picked as a teacher."

"It's true. For a second, I felt let down that I wasn't recognized. But then I realized that I will always be a student. That's how I will learn."

"But one of them was a young kid!"

"I can learn from young and old alike. Everyone has something to teach me if I am willing to listen."

The dark side makes a noise like a violin. "You'll have me crying if you keep it up. Sentimental crap, that's all it is. Sentimental CRAP!!!"

At home that evening, the woman tells Steve about beating the cushions. He says, "It's a load of bull shit! People shouldn't be that angry!"

"I wasn't ... but I have been, and anger has to come out somehow. It's better to beat a cushion than someone's head!"

"It's better not to have anger in the first place."

The woman's head reels—peace, anger, dark side all wanting attention. "I just want a happy life!" she says softly.

"Then have one," says Steve stroking her hair. "I love you very much," he adds.

"I love you too," she says snuggling into his chest. "I'm really happy with my life," she adds, wondering if she is.

The following day, the woman meets Silva and Shyam at Starbuck's coffee shop. They talk for a while and the woman says, "The only thing I haven't got a handle on is my weight!"

"Why is that?" asks Silva.

"Because she is a big fat cow!" says the dark side.

"Because I still overeat," says the woman. "I know diets don't work. I've tried exercising like an idiot. I've fasted. I've done everything, and I still get greedy when it comes to food."

"You're a glutton," says the dark side. "You want everything that everyone else has and more!"

"Can you visualize what the overeating looks like?" says Silva. "Maybe it looks like that garbage can out there." They all stare at the big, black, wrought iron cylinder standing outside the shop window.

"Maybe," says the woman.

"Yes. The garbage can is good. Smelly, full of rotting, sweaty, stale things that other people don't want," sniggers the dark side.

"I'm not sure, though." The woman has second thoughts. "How would that help me?"

"Every time you want to eat something, you should think of putting it in the garbage can instead."

"What a joke!" laughs the dark side.

"Hmmm!" says the woman unconvinced. "It's a greed thing yes, but where would I visualize the garbage can?"

"Kind of around you," says Shyam, spreading his arms open as if he has a large cylinder around his body.

"Hmmm." The woman is still unconvinced.

"What about using money?" says Silva, warming to the idea. "Every time you eat something you don't want, you could put money into something."

"That's interesting," says the woman, sitting forward on her stool. "I could have ten dollars at the beginning of the week, and every time I eat something I shouldn't eat, I throw a dollar away."

"That sounds great!" says Shyam.

"It does, doesn't it?" smiles the woman. "Wherever I am, I just throw a dollar away..."

"And someone who really needs it picks it up, and buys a cup of coffee or something."

"I'll get a special purse to use. I'll call it my *abundance purse.*"

"Great!" says Shyam, "but mom, you could throw the money in my direction also."

"Or mine!" says Silva.

"And as the money grows—because I am not going to throw much away—I can save it and do something really nice at the end."

"Brilliant!" says Silva.

At home she tells Steve her plan to lose weight. "You could call it your *fat bag,*" he laughs.

"This isn't funny," says the woman gravely.

"It won't work," says Steve. "Just stop eating! That's the only way to do it."

"I've tried that."

"No you haven't. If you had, you would be slim by now."

"I need something to remind me. My *abundance purse* will remind me not to eat foods that are bad for me."

"That purse will be gone by next week," says Steve, laughing. "You'll be in some restaurant wanting ice cream, and you'll look for your purse which you will have left at home, and you'll eat the ice cream."

"I will not."

"You will."

"I bet I keep the purse around me."

"I bet you can't even find it by next week!"

"And if I can, you have to take me to dinner!"

Steve splutters, "Oh great, we're talking slim and you reward yourself by eating out!"

"Okay, take me to a play downtown!"

"And if I win?"

"What do you want?"

"To take you into the Library and have your body behind the books."

"Yes, yes!" says the dark side remembering the last time they did that."

"I am never going to do that again!" says the woman.

"Why not?" asks Steve.

"What if someone had seen us? A little kid or something?"

"What's a kid doing in that part of the library? It's full of psychiatry, biographies and history."

"I was too scared. I am not doing it again."

"It depends on whether you lose the bet!"

The woman feels her fate is sealed. Lose weight, have sex in the library, or get used to being thin!

"Steve is right about the abundance purse or fat bag as he calls it. It won't work. You need to listen to me—I'm trying to tell you something and you won't listen." The dark side moans like a north wind approaching winter.

"Okay, tell me," says the woman.

"Feed yourself. Do things that make you happy. Feed your needs," says the dark side. "Diets and fat bags don't work."

"I hear what you're saying," says the woman. "I'm just not there yet. I don't really know what makes me happy. I don't know what can replace chocolate?"

"You do," says the dark side. "You just don't want to take responsibility for your happiness. It means being in the cockpit, taking the wheel and going for it 100%. It's easier to sit back and eat chocolate."

"Life is hard," says the woman.

"Life is what you make it," responds the dark side.

THE FEAR OF FEAR

There's a knife pointing straight at me. Its steel blade is sharp as a surgeon's eye. Death is indifferent as a raven's beak tearing at a road kill. Fearful and intrigued, I am both the dreamer and the silent witness.

Real time is 4:30AM. The bewitching hour of a freezing Chicago dawn breaks the night sky. Dream time. I am in an operating room of an English hospital. Nurses and surgeons, wrapped and tied against germs laugh at some innocuous joke. The baby on the table is me. "She's all yours!" says the anesthetist twiddling dials on giant gas bottles attached to plastic tubes that lead to the baby's face.

Terror invades my tiny body as ice-cold steel meets pink baby flesh and slits me open like a pomegranate. The blade is saving my life—hands reach in, straighten my twisted bowel and sew me up. In the Chicago bedroom, the 46-year-old scar lightens in color; skin releasing an imperceptible sigh.

I am propelled forward to the next knife. It is cutting into my six-year-old throat, whisking tonsils into a white enamel bowl. Forward to age 36; womb and ovaries removed and fragments of diseased cells isolated for biopsy; all I am left with is fear.

As the silent witness, I understand I must rid myself of this fear. I look for it inside my body and see a black hole in my belly. As soon as I locate it, the fear moves outside my body and I fling it toward a bright ball of sunlight. But there is more in the hole; nuts, bolts and all manner of black objects assemble there. As I cast them into the ball of light, more layers unfold, each worse than the one before.

Finally, a huge octopus-like creature emerges, its snake-like tentacles reach from my belly into my throat. Thoughts flood my mind, 'It's bigger than me! How can I rid myself of this monster? How did I create this?' I recite the Lord's prayer as I remember it, *'Our Father, who art in heaven, hallowed be Thy name. Thy*

Kingdom come, Thy will be done on earth as it is in heaven. Give us this day our daily bread and forgive us our trespasses as we forgive those who trespass against us. Lead us not into temptation but deliver us from evil, for Thine is the Kingdom, the power and the glory, for ever and ever, Amen.'

Reciting the prayer gives me the strength to send the creature to the light, and with it, the last remnants of fear.

Next morning, the woman writes in her dream journal and meditates on the meaning. Not totally discounting Freud's theory that knives are universally considered a penis symbol, or an activating force, the woman delves further into her mind. The knife image recalls The Ace of Swords from her Tarot pack. It means the seeds of success and triumph are now taking root. The beginning of something new, forgetting the past and putting energies into new ideas and plans.

She comes out of her meditation and looks up the Astrological meaning for the Ace of Swords and reads, Mercury-Capricorn-Saturn. Capricorn! The one sign she has so much trouble with. Mercury! Her own ruling planet! And Saturn, the cold planet of limitations and also the symbol of past karma!

From her astrology book, she reads, 'Saturn is truly the taskmaster but also our greatest friend because we learn and thus improve our life. Gains through Saturn are permanent; it is through Saturn that the useless, worn-out, old forms and things of life are destroyed so the new and more useful forms can replace them. The movement of Saturn is toward perfection.'

Everything fits into place. Yesterday, before the dream, the woman had taught her Tarot class about the Sword family. "Even though it can mean struggle and adversity, in ancient times, the sword was only given to those who had the strength to wield it," she told her group. "It is used to cut through obstacles, to point the way, to uphold the laws of the universe."

Yesterday afternoon, she had gone to Kate's house to give her knee a healing. Kate was in her kitchen looking pale and fragile. "It hurts so much. I couldn't get any sleep last night!"

"I brought you these." The woman puts the flowers into a blue vase and sits them on the dining room table.

"Thank you, they're beautiful. Oooh, I like your black velvet pants. I had a pair like those," says Kate. "I lost them."

"These are yours!" jokes the woman.

"You stole them when you took the tape," giggles Kate.

"That's right!" says the woman, glad they can joke about the tape now. "Okay, let's get down to business. Where do you want the healing?"

"Upstairs," says Kate, careful not to bend her knee as she gets up from the chair. "It seems so small a thing, but it aches so much!" She whimpers as she climbs the stairs to her bedroom.

"Lie down on the floor," instructs the woman, sitting at Kate's head so that she can rest her hands on either side of her temple. "Close your eyes and take a couple of deep breaths."

As she breathes out, the woman feels tension leave Kate's body and for the next twenty minutes she gives her Reike. "What do you see in your knee?"

"A black arrow," says Kate.

"Where are you?"

"I'm watching my father fight another tribe."

"How old are you?"

"Eight."

"Where is your mother?"

"She's looking after my other brothers and sisters, but that's okay, I want to be a warrior, I want to watch my father."

"What happens when the arrow strikes you?"

"I pull it out, but the shaft breaks off."

"Do you go to a doctor?"

"No. I am killed by another arrow."

"Why have you become aware of this arrow now, in this lifetime?"

"To remind me to be brave." Kate's face crumples and tears run down her face.

"It takes courage to be brave. Perhaps you can reconnect with the spirit of that young brave warrior, so you aren't alone?"

"I'd like that."

"Remember how you felt as that brave spirit. Open your solar plexus and bring that brave feeling into your body." The woman gives Kate a few moments to allow the visualization to take place. "How do you feel?"

Kate brings her hands up and rubs her face. "Wonderful."

"Is there anything else you need to get rid of?"

Kate thinks for a moment. "No," she answers.

The two women embrace and kiss each other on the cheek. The woman feels a deep happiness bubble up from inside. "Have I shown you my abundance purse?"

"Oh, I should put something in, shouldn't I?" asks Kate reaching for her own purse.

"No, no! I didn't mean that. I came here as a gift. I want to show you my purse." The woman holds the purse out for Kate to see. It is made from a soft lavender silk, with white flowers dotting the background. The shoulder strap is a group of long silken threads woven together in a cord.

"Let me put this in." Kate reaches inside her purse and brings out a clear, heart shaped crystal. "This was gifted to me by a very dear friend. I give it to you with love and friendship."

"Would you give it an abundance blessing too?"

Kate clasps the crystal between her palms. *"Lord of infinite light and love, may abundance, peace, love and health manifest forever and ever. Free her spiritual path from all difficulties and lead her to the shores of eternal wisdom and bliss. May Thy love and wisdom shine forever on the sanctuary of her soul. And may she be able to awaken Thy wisdom and love in all sentient creatures. Amen."* Kate hands the crystal to the woman who puts it carefully into her *abundance purse.*

"How did you sleep the night after Prashant gave us that incredible yoga class?" asks the woman.

"Wonderfully," says Kate. "I felt a deep healing take place. I slept like a baby."

"I didn't," said the woman. "I felt I didn't belong in my body. It was horrible, I tossed and turned all night long. And even the next day I felt bad."

"That's probably why you decided to lose weight," says Kate touching the *abundance purse.*

"My God, you're right!" says the woman. "I really do feel like my body doesn't fit me anymore. That I want to change it."

On her way home from Kate's, the woman bumps into a friend she has not seen for about a year. "Elena! How are you?"

"Fabulous. How are you?"

"Great!" The two women create a glow around one another as they talk.

"I finally accept that I am a healer," says Elena. "I've worked in my husband's business for so long, and it never felt right, but I

didn't know what to do. I still don't know what to do," she
laughs. "But I don't care. Something wonderful is going to happen, and I'm ready."

"I feel the same," says the woman. "I used to hate working
with Steve. I felt I could never do my writing; now, I'm able to
do it all. My days are filled with different things. I work on my
book, cook, clean, go for a walk, and other days I'm in the office
designing and writing training programs; I love it!"

"Aren't we lucky?"

"Blessed."

"Do you still go to the Temple?" asks Elena.

"Not as much as I should. In fact I have a real dilemma. Silva
is assisting at a workshop downtown, and I said I would attend.
It's the exact same time that my Guru is coming into town, and
I'm supposed to introduce him. It's a real honor!"

"Well of course you want to support your daughter," says
Elena, holding the woman's arm gently.

"I know, and yet I feel I should be with my Guru." The
woman kicks a leaf from the sidewalk. "And he's teaching
kundalini, which I really want to learn."

"I'm ordering that tape!" cries Elena. "I'm away that week-
end, so I've ordered it. You can borrow it!"

"I can?" The woman's face lights up as if under a key spot
light. "I couldn't afford the tape and go on this other workshop!"
The woman looks into Elena's eyes. "I can't believe it! I was
thinking about it only this morning. Worrying about what should
I do. And here you come along and solve it for me."

"The universe has a way of helping us out," says Elena
smiling.

Later that day, the woman is talking to Jenny, the one who is
doing all the body work on herself. "I haven't talked to you for
ages," says the woman.

"Why haven't you called?" asks Jenny. "I'm not saying that
as a negative thing, I was just wondering."

"I've been busy, writing my book, working; life is wonderful."

"Not for me, it isn't," says Jenny. "I've got a new therapist
and it's bringing up a lot of things. I realize I have been stuffing
my emotions and feelings into my body for years."

"But you knew that already," says the woman.

"On an intellectual level I did, but now I'm really feeling it," says Jenny. "My body is in a lot of pain too!"

"When will you be through?" asks the woman.

"I don't know!" Irritation creeps into Jenny's voice. "How do I know how long a thing like this will take?"

"It's just that I remember you telling me what your grandmother always said." The woman waits for a response and when there is none she continues. "That you could get anything you wanted."

"Do anything I put my mind to!" corrects Jenny.

"Why not say to yourself that you will be healed in two months?"

Jenny laughs as if to a small child. "I don't know about that. It's not that easy."

"Why not?" The woman really doesn't know what she's talking about but continues her thought. "How does a shrink work with a patient anyway? Patients are their source of income; it makes sense for them to drag it out as long as possible. It's an oxymoron for them; heal the patient and kill the income!"

The woman remembers a friend saying, "The problem is, too many aluminum-siding-type people are marketing the spiritual stuff! All they're interested in is money!" The friend mimicked a soft, squelchy ad-type voice, "A crystal a day keeps the doctor away! Decide your fate with a feather! People don't realize it takes self-discipline. They should focus on one thing instead of doing every workshop in sight!"

The woman returns her mind to the conversation with Jenny, "Maybe your own power and strength can help you process the stuff through much quicker!"

"Ha, ha, ha, I don't know about that. I think it has it's own time," laughs Jenny.

The conversation ends and the woman thinks about a program she saw on TV called *Front Line*. It scared her. It was about MPD (Multiple Personality Disorders) and Satanic Cults. She wondered if her dark side was an undiagnosed Multiple Personality Disorder!

The program featured a doctor at a Chicago hospital. He'd taken a woman into psychiatric care and diagnosed her with MPD. Video showed the woman held down by various nurses who told her she was a victim of a Satanic Cult. That she had probably eaten human flesh and performed other vile things. The woman's life was torn apart, her husband and son left her and it wasn't until five years later when she saw another psychiatrist that she finally pulled herself together.

It was as if the doctor was a Satanic Cult member, not the patient! The woman being interviewed said, "The new doctor told me that if I wanted the multiple voices in my head to go away, I could just do it. So I did! I never realized I had any control over them! It was like being set free!"

Later, the woman discussed the program with another friend who said, "Satanic Cults *do* exist. That woman was just very susceptible to what other people told her."

The program caused the woman to have a lurking fear within. She tells Steve about it. "What if I can't get rid of the dark side?"

"So?" said Steve.

"I have to live with it?"

"Maybe," says Steve, waiting for the other shoe to drop.

"It could haunt me for the rest of my life!"

"How is it now?" asks Steve.

"It's disappeared!" says the woman after a few moments. "I haven't heard it for quite some time," she says, wondering if it is going to 'pop up' and shriek verbal abuse at her.

"So it's gone, and if it comes back, it's okay too," says Steve warmly.

"Why?"

"Because you know how to deal with it." He continues as if they are talking about reordering a can of beans.

"That's true," says the woman, feeling more calm. Weeks later she is lying in bed and reviewing her life: The pain in her left side has definitely gone. She knows she does not have cancer. Her abundance purse is full of money, she has lost 20 pounds and she hasn't been on a diet!

Next week, she is writing a training program for a billion dollar communications company and getting paid $20,000 for it. Money is definitely flowing in. She has gone from being a 15 to a 150 watt light bulb! Her skin glows, her hair shines and laughter bubbles up in almost every conversation she has.

"Excuse me?" The dark side has been silent as of late.

"Yes," says the woman.

"Where do I fit in?"

"Where would you like to fit in?" she asks gently.

"I don't know. I feel lost, as if I can't have a normal conversation with you any more," complains the dark side.

"I asked if we could be friends, and you said no. I haven't any room for anything else."

"Do I hang around in limbo?"

"Think of it as a good, long rest. When I need you again..." The woman rephrases it, "If I need you again, I'll call."

"I'll be here," says the dark side.

The woman watches her dark side disappear. It doesn't go to lurk in some dark corner, it simply fades away as if it never existed. And the fact that she can call it back again if she needs to is comforting. As if she has an ego trimmer at her disposal. Someone who wants her empty of anything that may hold her back from being the best that she can be.

She looks round her writing room and thinks about how far she has come in such a short space of time. She glances over her books and one title stands out from the rest: *Apprentice!* That's what she is, an apprentice of life, always open for more knowledge, both the teacher and the student. "AHAM-BRAHMASMI," she says quietly to the room, *"I am the creative principle."*

"OM SHANTIH, SHANTIH, SHANTIH." The room echoes back, *Peace, Peace, Peace!*

"And everyone lives happily ever after! What a load of bull shit!" The dark side knows better.

"For God's sake, can't you keep quiet and let the book end on a positive note!" says the woman more calmly than she feels.

"What would be the point?" continues the dark side. "Is this a true story or what?"

"Half and half," says the woman, wondering if it qualifies as non-fiction.

"It is about you isn't it?"

"Yes. But I renamed the other characters so I don't get sued."

"Have you really lost 20lbs?" asks the dark side already knowing the answer.

"Not exactly."

"Why did you say it then?"

"Because I am losing weight. I have the self-discipline. I'm learning from the animals and birds. They eat simple, natural food and never have to go to the doctor. They don't need pills for constipation or insomnia, or to get rid of gas. It's because they live according to nature."

"You don't have the will-power of a flea!"

"My addiction to over-eating weakened my will, the more I ate, the more I needed—but I don't crave food anymore. I've never felt happier in my whole life."

"Good for you dunder-breath," says the dark side. "As long as you know that we will meet again."

"I know!" smiles the woman. "For now though, Good night— sleep tight!"

"Good night, fatso!" says the dark side slinking off to its corner. "Have a doughnut why don't you?"

"No thanks—sweet dreams!"

The dark side does not answer—and the woman feels heroic. She has faced her fears and knows that although they still exist and will probably never leave, the fear of the fear has been conquered.

"What a dufus!" sneers the dark side.

"You're so right," agrees the woman smiling.

ABOUT THE AUTHOR

Shanti Ananda is an ordained Swami Priest and a Certified teacher of Hatha Yoga. She is a Reiki healer and uses guided imagery and visualization techniques with her students. Born in England in 1949, Shanti Ananda traveled extensively before coming to the United States in 1983. She has been married for over twenty-seven years and has two daughters. She and her husband founded their own company in 1988, designing and facilitating workshops for major corporations throughout the world. This is her first published work.

An Excerpt From Shanti Ananda's 'Conversations With My Light Side'

[If you liked *Conversations With My Dark Side,* you won't want to miss Shanti Ananda's companion book, *Conversations With My Light Side.* Here's a preview.]

Bleached hair lies dead in the sink. Grasping short clumps, the woman cuts as close to her scalp as she can without drawing blood.

"What are you doing?" laughs the light side.

"Chopping off my hair!" replies the woman.

"Why?"

"Because I need to be liberated."

"Why?"

"I just do." Shortly before, the woman sat in her bath tub sobbing tears as big as quarters. They mix with foaming surge around her breasts and knees, white-capped like Mount Everest. "Dear God," she asks. "What can I do?"

"Shave your head," says a voice no bigger than a cats whisker.

"That can't be God's voice. God wouldn't ask me to do anything so silly."

"It is a bit radical," agrees the light side. "Still ... be it on your own head."

The dilemma arose when her son called the office earlier that day, "Mom, I've totaled the car."

"You've what?" says the woman.

"Take a short breath or three," laughs the light side.

Pause. "Tell me you're joking," she says.

"I'm not joking mom."

"But how...?"

"I fell asleep."

"You what!!"

"We were bumper to bumper and I fell asleep. Next thing I'm in the back of this other car."

"What the fuck!" The woman's anger rises like an electric storm on a full moon. "What were you thinking?"

"Don't ask me if I'm okay or anything."

For a brief second, maternal instincts get the better of her. "Are you?"

"A bit of whiplash, but I'm still intact."

Maternal check over, the woman resumes anger status, "I can't believe you fucking did this."

"It's okay mom. I showed the police the insurance, and it's all taken care of."

"We don't have insurance!"

"Sure we do. The papers are in the glove compartment."

"The insurance has lapsed."

"But the papers are there … the dates and everything."

"Trust me. It was the wrong insurance. We're in the middle of applying for different coverage. We're not insured."

Like grave robbers their silence is palpable. "I'm sorry mom."

"Just tell me what to do," says the woman. "Tell me what I'm supposed to do, because I don't know what to do."

Her son changes phone hands and inadvertently presses the key pad. Wild discordant beeps trill into the woman's ear. "Tell me what to do?" She shouts.

"I'll call the other driver and see if we can pay for the damage."

"We don't have the money," the woman looks at the carpet, the ceiling, the windows, the walls. Everything remains standing, while her mind crumbles like frost-bitten cement. "Every time I think we're getting it together, something happens."

"I'll pay for it mom."

"How can you? You don't have a full-time job."

"I'll get one."

"Call the other driver of the car, and call me back." The phone clicks. She holds it immobile in her hand. *"If you'd like to make a call, please hang up and try again. If you need help, hang up and then dial your operator."* Doubting the operator can help in this situation, the woman puts the phone back safely in its cradle.

After half an hour of looking into deep space, she searches for a pigeonhole—which in this case is the bath tub.

The next day...

"Get your little buns over here," laughs the light side.

"Excuse me?"

"Sit down and write, don't give me no fight. Be the best, get it off your chest."

"Write what?"

"Whatever I say, what time of day. Write down the word, don't be a nerd."

The woman has just finished meditating and has asked her light side to come through. She has been too manipulative in writing the voice of the light side—too much of her. She has asked people the same question, "What is a light side?" No one seems to know.

Her daughter's friend. Angel said, "You need to go deeper." Easy for you to say, thinks the woman.

Steve says his light side is like a comedian spewing one-liners. "It sees the funny side in everything, even the really bad things. I have to constantly censure myself."

"How do you mean?" asks the woman.

"Remember when we went to see Diedre in hospital last year?" he says.

The woman recalls muted voices bouncing off yellow walls, steel bed frames on polished floors, clear, plastic tubes sucking in and out of flesh and the smell of boiled, sterile sheets. "Yes," she says.

"I kept imagining a nurse coming in and sticking a huge bunch of flowers in her bum."

"That's awful," says the woman. "She was dying!"

"Yes but she was on her tummy, moments away from death and her bum just reminded me of a flower vase."

"But death is serious."

"It shouldn't be," says Steve. "It should be celebrated. I really believe we go on to somewhere much better."

The woman inhales the thought. "Is the light side like Robin Williams then?" she asks.

"I don't know," he says. "It's funny that your dark side came through so easily, and you're having trouble with the light side."

"I was just thinking the same thing!" she says laughing.

Now this morning, a rap voice is coming through, which she still thinks is contrived. The woman has expected her light side to be heavenly, like angel wings fluttering between breaths. Short, easy sentences, carried softly on warm, honey sweet air.

"Too flowery for me, get real and be the woman you are, you could go far."

"Excuse me?" The woman does not know how to continue the book. She has completed chapters. Should she go back and redo them?

"No, no, no. I couldn't bear it!" Her light screams with laughter.

"Then what?" She asks.

"Keep going and see what happens."

"Should I continue with the story about my shaved head?"

"Sounds good to me."

"So here I am, shaving my head," says the woman. "The job is more difficult than I imagine." Eight pink lady-razors later, my scalp is crisscrossed like a topography map charting rivers, and mountainous regions of rain forest. In half-an-hour I'm picking up Steve from the airport. "What the hell can I wear to hide my head?"

"A baseball cap?" suggests her light side.

The woman tries this and stares at her reflection. She has just finished putting together an outline for a noon meditation at her Temple entitled, *HAIL TO YOUR OWN REFLECTION!* She doesn't feel much to **Hail** about at the moment. "It's okay for the Dalai Lama to wear a shaved head, he's got the robes to go with the look, but me?"

"You could make something out of drapes like Scarlet O'Hara in *Gone With The Wind,* chortles the light side.

"You're not much help," gasps the woman. "I look like a conehead."

"Wear earrings," suggests the light side with a giggle. She puts a long, dangly, silver crystal in each ear lobe and stands back. "There you go! Accessorized Buddhist."

Driving to O'Hare with the windows open, the woman takes off her baseball cap to feel the wind on her shaved head. Missing, is the sensation of rippling hair. The man at the toll booth smiles sympathetically and says, "Have a nice day!"

"He thinks I'm on chemo," laughs the woman.

"Probably," chortles the light side.

At arrivals, Steve waves, opens the back car door, slings his luggage in and climbs in the front. The woman drives off, knuckles tense on the steering wheel, no kisses yet. "You've shaved your head?" he laughs uneasily.

"Yep!" she replies.

"As soon as I saw the baseball cap, I knew," They focus on speeding black tarmac, car plates, hard shoulder. "What made you do it?"

The woman tells him about their son's car accident, finishing with, "So I was crying in the bath, thinking I don't have a real job; I don't make any money writing; I should get back into the corporate world ... when I heard a voice say, *'shave your head!'*"

"So you couldn't go back into corporate," laughs Steve.

"And I realized how lucky I am that our son is okay. And how horrible I was to swear and react in such a bad way. I felt liberated."

"So you shaved your head," Steve laughs.

"I want a new beginning," she looks at him now. "To cut off the old and start anew." Feeling his eyes upon her, she takes the cap off and shrinks into her body. "What do you think?"

"Good," he says.

"You still love me?"

"Of course."

"Even though I'm bald?"

"Even bald."

"Do you think I'm crazy?"

"You are crazy!"

The woman thinks about this for a moment. "You really think I'm crazy?"

"Yes!"

"Yes, I suppose I am." The thought worries her.

The light side laughs, "You're worried that God told you to shave your head, and that if God asks you to kill yourself, you will!"

"Right."

"God never asks anyone to harm themselves."

"Did God tell me to shave my head?" she asks.

"Maybe, maybe not," laughs the light side. "Does it matter?"

"Not really."

"Well then."

Back home, Steve looks at her head, "You need to shave it more evenly. I'll do it if you like."

"I'm not sure," she laughs nervously.

"Please yourself."

Looking at her moth eaten scalp she says, "Promise not to cut me."

Steve looks into her eyes like a wolf, clear and sharp focused. "Promise," he says. The woman helps him unpack his bags to find the steel razor.

"Be careful!" she wails.

"Sit still." Steve lathers her head and shaves. She hears the razor scrape across her scalp and feels green bile rise up from her stomach. After he's finished, she drags herself to bed.

"Are you okay?" Steve peers into her ashen face.

"I feel faint," she whimpers. "I'll be fine after a good nights rest."

"I'll get you some water," Steve tucks the blankets around her. Returning with the glass he makes her sip, "I hate it when you aren't feeling well."

"Why?"

"When you're not well, the world looks dark."

"I think I'll hide away until it's grown back," she says.

"I thought the idea was to be liberated."

"I don't have the guts to go through with it."

"You already have," smiles Steve.

"Oh right," she repeats. "I have, haven't I!"

CONVERSATIONS
The Source to Change Your Life. Create:

- Money
- Security
- Happiness
- Love
- Truth

Each month you will receive an eight page study guide—complete with tools to help you create a sense of well-being and leave you feeling **EMPOWERED.**

Subscribe *now* and let Shanti Ananda guide you through the steps that unlock your true potential and enhance your self-esteem. Locate your spiritual center through reasoning and intuition. This study guide is startling and ingenious in its effectiveness..

Complete the form below and mail to:

Shanti Ananda, PO Box 645, Lake Forest, Illinois 60045 USA

Yes, I would like to give myself a subscription to **Conversations.**

_____
NAME (AS YOU WISH IT TO APPEAR ON MAILING. PLEASE UNDERLINE SURNAME.)

_____
ADDRESS

_____
CITY/STATE/COUNTRY   ZIP/POSTAL CODE

☐ One year (U.S.$90) ☐ Two years ($155) ☐ Three years ($210)

☐ Check/MO (U.S. funds) enclosed, payable to: **Shanti Ananda**

☐ Please charge to my credit card:

☐ American Express ☐ Visa ☐ Master Card

Card # ☐☐☐☐☐☐☐☐☐☐☐☐☐☐☐☐☐☐☐

Expiration Date: Month: ☐☐ Year: ☐☐

_____
SIGNATURE (AS SHOWN ON CARD)   DATE

_____
PLEASE PRINT NAME HERE.